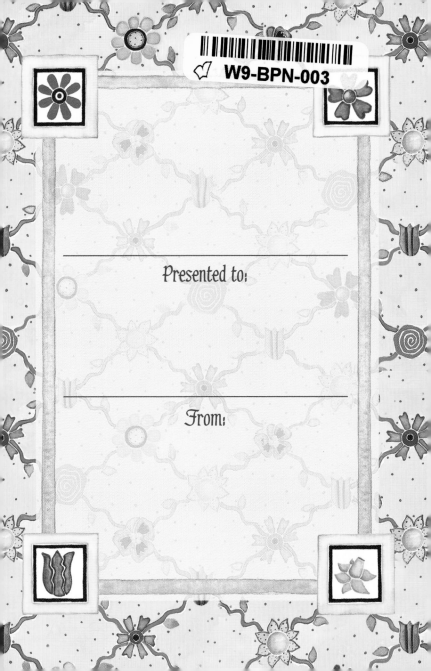

Presented to:

From:

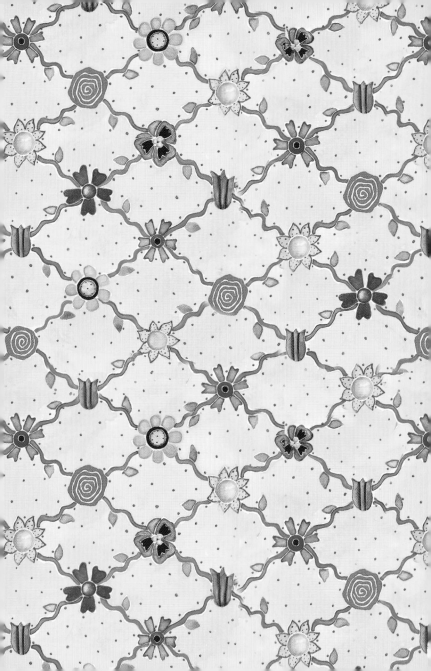

Simple Words of Wisdom

52 Virtues for Every Woman

Penelope J. Stokes

COUNTRYMAN®

Simple Words of Wisdom

Copyright © 1998 by Penelope J. Stokes

Illustrations copyright © 1998 by Michelle Allen

Published by J. Countryman™ a Division of Thomas Nelson, Inc., Nashville, Tennessee 37214.

Managing Editor—Terri Gibbs

J. Countryman is a registered trademark of Thomas Nelson Inc.

A J. Countryman™ Book

Designed by Garborg Design Works, Minneapolis, Minnesota

ISBN: 08499-5408-8

Printed in Hong Kong

CONTENTS

Foreword

PART 1
The Private Virtues

PART 2
The Public Virtues

Foreword

Virtue is becoming fashionable again. Angels populate the airways; priests and pastors fill the silver screen in both comedy and drama. Honor, nobility, even faith, bring out the warm fuzzies in people.

But what is virtue? Is it just the nice feeling we get when we've done a random act of kindness? Is it something we can acquire, the way we learn table manners and proper social conduct?

Jesus didn't think so. In Mark 5, a woman with an issue of blood pushes her way through the crowd to touch the hem of the Master's garment. Instantly she finds herself healed, and in that moment, the Scripture tells us, Jesus perceives "that virtue had gone out of him" (Mark 5:30, KJV).

Virtue is power.

Not the kind of power that lords it over others and oppresses them, but a healing, restorative power that enables us to live in hope and joy and love.

True virtue, the reflection of Christlikeness, cannot be accomplished by human effort. It stems from something far deeper—an inner change that can only be accomplished by the Spirit of God.

The purpose of this book is not to teach readers to act virtuously, but to encourage us all to seek God's transforming power for our inner lives. The private virtues—those hidden wellsprings of faith that center in our secret relationship with God—form the foundation for the public virtues, those attitudes of compassion and acts of love that govern our relationships with those around us.

The path toward Christlikeness is a lifelong journey, a journey that changes us as we submit ourselves to the work of the Spirit along the way. It is my prayer that as you contemplate these virtues, you will find your soul drawn into a deeper relationship with God, who is the source of all virtue and the Author and Finisher of our faith.

Penelope J. Stokes

PART
1

The
Private
Virtues

Authenticity

Nature forever puts a premium on reality.
—Emerson, 1860

I received an offer in the mail the other day—an opportunity to purchase, at a greatly reduced price, a strand of "genuine faux pearls." I've seen this ploy before: an office chair covered in "genuine Naugahyde," as if some poor "nauga" had given his life for my seat cover. A solitaire of "authentic cubic zirconia."

We live in a world of genuine fakes, authentic reproductions, bona fide imitations. But God—our genuine, unique, unadulterated Lord—calls us to something more than the appearance of authenticity.

When Jesus was choosing his disciples, he came upon Nathanael and exclaimed, "Here is truly an Israelite, in whom there is nothing false" (John 1:47).

Most of us, if Christ were to give us such a compliment,

would hang our heads, put on a semblance of humility, and protest, "Aw, not me, Lord."

Nathanael's response was more straightforward: "How do you know me?"

Jesus responded, "I saw you while you were still under the fig tree before Philip called you."

I saw you, Jesus' words imply, *when you didn't know I was watching. I saw you alone, with no one to impress, no image to maintain. I saw the reality of your deepest soul. You are who you claim to be.*

Authenticity is a hallmark of true faith, a living demonstration of the belief that God knows us as we are. We can't hide from God. We can't fool the Spirit. The Lord created us, redeemed us, understands us.

We can't masquerade as something we're not.

With Christ, we have nothing to hide. We don't need to camouflage ourselves in a mantle of spirituality, the way Adam and Eve tried to cover their nakedness. We are revealed. We are loved. We are forgiven. We don't have to pretend any more.

Authenticity with God and within our own souls brings great liberty, and great power. We can relax and be ourselves. We can admit our shortcomings and allow God to work within us. We can stop trying to keep up a front and let the Spirit come in. And then a miraculous transformation begins to occur. We begin to look more like Jesus.

Balance

Genius is formed in quiet;
character in the stream of human life.

— Goethe, 1790

Years ago, I hid behind a display of potato chips and watched in fascination as one of my college professors—by all reports a rather stuffy, conventional fellow—juggled lemons in the produce aisle of our local supermarket. He was good at it, too. He could keep four lemons in the air, his eyes watching the flying fruit, never once glancing at his hands.

Juggling—when it's done with lemons or oranges or rubber balls or bowling pins—can be an amusing pastime. But the modern world presents us with a more dangerous kind of juggling, the kind involving flaming torches and razor-sharp knives. Sometimes we feel as if our life depends on our juggling skills: husband, wife, children, parents, friends, relatives, family time, money, spiritual growth, church responsibilities, community service, jobs, bosses, recreation. Everything is important; everything vies for our attention. If we lose our rhythm for an instant, chaos ensues.

But God does not call us to be jugglers. God calls us to be people of *balance.*

Martha, in the Bible, was an accomplished juggler—if she had lived in our generation, her last name probably would have been Stewart. When Jesus brought his disciples to her home, Martha scurried around fixing dinner, setting the table, creating a nice centerpiece, making sure everything was just perfect. Mary, Martha's sister, didn't get in on the circus routine. Instead, she sat at the Master's feet and listened to what he was saying.

Finally, Martha began to lose her rhythm. Her juggling act was falling apart, and she panicked. "Lord," she said to Jesus, "don't you care that my sister has left me to do the work by myself? Tell her to help me!" (Luke 10:40)

But Jesus had a different agenda, one that didn't include juggling unnecessary details. He responded: "Martha, Martha, you are worried and upset about many things, but only one thing is needed. Mary has chosen what is better, and it will not be taken away from her" (41-42).

Does God care about all the responsibilities we have to juggle in our daily lives? Of course. But he cares more that our lives demonstrate *balance*, the ability to discern what is essential and give ourselves fully to it. "Only one thing is needed," Jesus said, "and Mary has chosen it."

Our spiritual life, our connection with God, is the foundational relationship around which everything else revolves. It is the solid footing that enables us to fulfill our responsibilities, the bedrock that provides stability for the construction of our lives.

We may be able to *juggle* a lot of things at once, but we can only *hold* a few things at a time.

Our Lord. Our loved ones. Our inner lives. Our outward calling.

Commitment

A piece of incense may be as large as the knee but, unless burnt, emits no fragrance.
— Malay Proverb

New Year's Day has come and gone. People are talking about their resolutions: go on a diet, walk two miles a day, get organized, clean out the hall closet, spend more time with the family, give more attention to devotions and prayer.

Promises, promises.

Talk, as the old adage says, is cheap. It's now two weeks into the new year, and most of those resolutions have already gone into the recycling bin. The spirit may be willing, but the flesh just can't seem to keep up. We mean well, we really do. We fully intend to keep those promises, this time. But before long "this time" becomes just like all the other times. We slip back into our old comfortable patterns.

Why is it so difficult for us to keep the commitments we make? Perhaps because the changes we seek are external rather than internal. We can make vows to God and to others until Jesus comes, but unless true commitment is rooted deep in our hearts, we are bound to fail, to disappoint our loved ones and ourselves.

We live in a society where lack of commitment is the accepted norm. If the road to marital bliss gets a little rocky, bail out and start over with someone new. If a job's tougher than you planned, turn it over to someone else—or just abdicate it altogether. If you're always late for appointments—hey, no big deal. They'll wait.

No wonder we have trouble keeping our word. No wonder our zeal flags and our determination fades. Commitment, in the modern world, simply isn't a very high priority.

To God, however, commitment is the very bedrock of faith. And it begins, not with our external efforts to change our outward patterns, but with a profound inward conviction that draws us into a commitment to Someone greater than ourselves.

"How can I repay the Lord for all his goodness to me?" the Psalmist asks. "I will lift up the cup of salvation and call upon the name of the Lord. I will fulfill my vows to the Lord in the presence of all his people" (Ps. 116:12-14).

When we commit our lives to God, something happens deep within us. Our priorities begin to change. We begin to see the spiritual truth in everyday life, to realize that keeping our word is not just a matter of making a good impression, but a matter of being true to the One who created us and redeemed us, the One in whose image we have been reborn.

Commitment is not an outward effort, but an inner transformation.

It's not a New Year's resolution; it's a gift of grace.

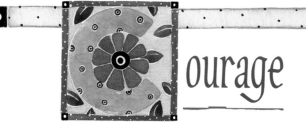

ourage

*Courage is resistance to fear, mastery of fear
—not absence of fear.*

—Mark Twain, 1894

Helen is a woman of great courage. Debilitated by Multiple Sclerosis and Lyme disease, demoralized by constant financial pressure, daunted by perpetual pain and depression, she just keeps going. She doesn't give in. And even in the midst of difficulties that would break most people, she discovers love and laughter, faith and hope.

Is Helen afraid? Does she fear what the future holds? Undoubtedly. But she doesn't let her life be ruled by it. Instead, she finds reason, one day at a time, to keep on living.

"I am confident of this," David says in Psalm 27: "I will see the goodness of the Lord in the land of the living" (Ps. 27:13).

Yet David had plenty of reason not to be so confident. Enemies were seeking his life;

evil people had risen up to challenge him. He was besieged on every side by opposition. And yet he says—to himself, and to all who seek God: "Wait for the Lord; be strong and take heart" (Ps. 27:14).

Most of us don't face enemies on the battlefield or incurable diseases or threats to our lives on a daily basis. But all of us live with fear.

Does my spouse really love me? Are my kids in trouble?

Can I muster the courage to leave an abusive relationship?

Is my job secure? Should I take the risk to change careers?

Legitimate fears, all of them. Fears we see confirmed every night on the national and local news. Fears that invade our dreams and consume our waking hours.

Life demands courage. But courage is not a blissful denial of reality. It is not the adrenaline kick that enables us to skydive or bungee-jump. It is not a bequest from the Wizard of Oz that empowers all of us Cowardly Lions to be suddenly and irreversibly brave.

Courage is the conviction that we will see the goodness of the Lord in the land of the living. No matter what life brings to us, we can rise above our fears. We can trust God to be our light and our salvation, the stronghold of our lives.

Devotion

God enters by a private door into every individual.
— Ralph Waldo Emerson, 1841

Years ago, as a young Christian trying to find my way with God, I attended a seminar entitled, "Managing Your Devotional Life." The seminar leader spent two days teaching us how to "have devotions"—how to set aside daily time for prayer and meditation on the Word, how to plan a schedule and stick to it, how to keep a devotional journal.

It was helpful information, but it didn't answer the deeper question burning in my newly converted heart: *What does it mean to be devoted to God?*

The religious disciplines—prayer, Bible study, worship, meditation, fellowship—have value, of course, in the quest to know God better. But what we *do* can never substitute for who we *are*, on the inside, in the secret places that only God sees. The inner virtue of devotion is ultimately a private matter, between you and God.

Let's face it—when you fall in love, your time with your beloved is not limited to a prearranged schedule: fifteen minutes to touch base in the morning, lunch twice a week, and an extended date for a couple of hours on the weekend. Whether you're together or apart, throughout the day your thoughts drift to the one you love. The sound of your beloved's voice brings a smile to your lips and a quiver to your stomach. When your loved one enters the room, your face lights up. Your beloved is the last thought on your mind as you fall asleep and your first memory upon waking. That dear countenance invades your dreams and leaves you breathless.

So it is when we fall in love with Christ.

"O God, you are my God," David says. "Earnestly I seek you; my soul thirsts for you.... Because your love is better than life, my lips will glorify you. I will praise you as long as I live, and in your name I will lift up my hands" (Ps. 63:1-4).

This is devotion. No scheduled list of activities can ever take the place of such all-consuming love.

And lest you're tempted to argue that David was a special case, God's anointed, a "man after God's own heart," remember David's darker side: He was a murderer, an adulterer. A sinner.

Just like you and me.

True devotion to God isn't some special grace given to saints and prophets. It is adoration, pure and simple. Adoration beyond ritual, beyond discipline, beyond schedules and timetables and appointments with God.

Devotion to the Lord is your soul reaching out and finding God's heart reaching back.

Endurance

It was the final hour, the moment of truth. The women's gymnastics team could, with one clean vault, take home Olympic gold for the first time. The world held its breath as a tiny slip of a girl named Kerri Strug began her run. She hit the springboard, vaulted, and then...

Her ankle twisted under her, and she went down. It looked as if all hope was lost.

Kerri Strug, however, had inner resources no one had counted on. Limping, and in obvious agony, she went back for her second vault, landed beautifully, and brought home the gold—on a broken ankle.

It's was the ultimate test of physical endurance.

But you don't have to train for the Olympics to have the virtue of endurance. Other kinds of endurance are equally valuable, although perhaps not so publicly acclaimed: the stamina to hang in there

16

with a rebellious teenager and help him turn his life around; the fortitude to weather a difficult storm in your marriage without giving up; the determination to finish your college degree even if you're the oldest person at graduation; the ability to hold onto your faith during a long dark night of the soul.

Whether you're expending the effort for the gold medal, your relationships, your education, or your spiritual life, the virtue of endurance is based on *love*. Love of the game. Love of your spouse or child. Love of learning. Love of God. "Love," First Corinthians 13:7 says, "bears all things, believes all things, hopes all things, endures all things. Love never fails."

Athletes, who are experts in physical endurance, often talk about "pushing through the pain." You don't stop running because you're winded or exhausted or have a stitch in your side or a cramp in your calf. You keep going, knowing that somehow, at the end of the race, the pain will be worth the prize.

So it is in our spiritual lives. When adversities come—and make no mistake, they *will* come—the person of endurance keeps going. When the relationship seems hopelessly bogged down in trivial matters, when the outcome just doesn't seem worth the effort, when God is silent and the night grows dark, we push beyond the pain and look ahead to the finish line. We hold on. We endure. We trust.

And we discover—perhaps not in the short run, but eventually—that God is still there, even when we do not hear the Divine Whisper in our ears.

Flexibility

An unexpected snowstorm came last week — heavy and wet, taking down power lines and telephone connections under its weight. Branches fell. Trees snapped in half like toothpicks, blocking the highways and causing accidents. But some of the trees, miraculously, survived. They bowed low to the ground under the burden. Then when the sun came out and the snow began to melt, they stood upright again — a little battered by the wear, but whole. They bent, so they did not break.

One of the hallmarks of a mature, solid faith is flexibility. Let's face it — things don't always go the way we'd like them to,

even when we're seeking to live our lives in obedience to God. Prayers are not always answered in the way we want, or when we want. God seems to hold out on us, to delay.

Perhaps the Lord is trying to teach us to be a little more flexible.

Luke's Gospel tells the story of a religious man's encounter with the Messiah — a man named Jairus, a ruler of the synagogue (Luke 8:40-56). Jairus's twelve-year-old daughter was dying, and he came to the Master to ask for help. But as Jesus was on his way to Jairus's house to heal the little girl, he was delayed by a woman with an issue of blood. The poor woman had been hemorrhaging for twelve years—since the very year Jairus's little daughter had been born.

If I had been Jairus, seeking Christ for the life of my child, I probably would have fought for my place in line. First come, first served—I had dibs on the Master's attention. But the Gospel gives no indication of impatience from Jairus, or from Jesus either, for that matter. Christ was flexible—willing to delay his mission in order to offer grace and love to a woman who needed him. And Jairus, too, demonstrated a remarkable level of compliance—waiting, trusting, even when his servants came to tell him that because of the delay, his little girl was dead.

Often we praise the firm, unyielding virtues—a willingness to stand up for what we believe, a rock-solid faith, an unwavering integrity. But sometimes we need to bend. We need to let go of our preconceived notions of what we believe and how God is supposed to work in our lives. We need to open ourselves to the possibility that delay, too, might be part of God's plan, that the Lord is not bound by our time restrictions or our self-imposed limitations.

Jairus's daughter died. But then—an even more astounding miracle than the promised healing—Jesus brought her back to life again!

When our dreams die, when storms threaten to shatter our resolve, when our faith wavers in the face of unanticipated difficulty, we needn't panic. Flexibility, too, is a virtue, a reflection of the nature of God being formed in us.

You can't stop the wind from blowing. But you can let the Lord teach you how to bend.

Forgiveness

It's a staple of modern drama—the emotional agony of betrayal. One particularly memorable scene from the recent film *Waiting to Exhale* grips the soul with its power and poignancy. A woman, victimized by her husband's infidelity, gathers up his clothes, his shoes, his personal belongings, and stuffs them into his expensive Mercedes. When the closets and drawers are empty, she returns to the car, sets a torch to the contents, and stands there with tears streaming down her cheeks as the evidence of her marriage goes up in flames.

Most people in the audience cheered. I cried, because her defiant gesture of closure did nothing to heal the woundedness of her heart.

As long as we are human, we will inevitably experience the agony of personal betrayal. People let us down, hurt us, disappoint us—sometimes deliberately, sometimes inadvertently. By the very nature of life in a fallen world, we have to confront the anguish of infidelity, faithlessness, indifference—all those wounds of the spirit that threaten to take us under. Sooner or later we all have to come to grips

20

with the issue of forgiveness.

But true forgiveness, biblical forgiveness, is not an external accomplishment, a white-knuckled, force-yourself-to-do-it-whether-you-like-it-or-not act of imposed self-righteousness. When Jesus, dining in the house of Simon the Pharisee, forgave the sins of the woman who anointed his feet, he explained to his host the nature of real forgiveness: "Her sins, which were many, have been forgiven; hence she has shown great love. But the one to whom little is forgiven, loves little" (Luke 7:47-48).

Forgiveness that extends outward to others begins inwardly, in the heart. It begins with comprehending how deeply we ourselves *need* to be forgiven.

The woman who anointed Jesus' feet understood this. She was conscious of her sins, aware of her unrighteousness before God. She knew her need. And when her sins were forgiven, she responded with an outpouring of love so great that it shamed those who called themselves followers of the Messiah.

In the Lord's prayer, Jesus set forth a radical pattern for living: "Forgive our sins, as we forgive those who sin against us." The key to "forgiving as we have been forgiven," I believe, lies in spiritual self-awareness, acknowledging just how much mercy we need—and have received—from the Lord. If I am mindful, on a daily basis, that the sinless Christ endured death on the cross for my sins, I'm likely to be less judgmental and more forgiving toward those who cause me pain.

Forgiveness is not so much an action as an attitude—a virtue of the heart. A perspective of gratefulness toward God and love toward others.

Godliness

There is one spectacle grander than the sky, that is the interior of the soul.

~ Victor Hugo, 1862

Those ancient family photos tell the tale: my ancestors in sepia tones, peering out at me from the cracking pages of an album that dates back to the Civil War. I don't know their names, but I know they trace their lineage from the Stokes clan. Heavy overhanging brows, dark eyes, square jowls that become more pronounced with age—even with the dilution of generations, those dominant genes prevail. The family resemblance is remarkable.

I pray that, as I mature, the "family resemblance" that marks me as a daughter of God will be equally evident.

For that is what we're called to, after all—to take on the characteristics of the One who created us in the Divine Image. The prime directive of spiritual life is not what we *do*, but who we *are*. It is the passion to become increasingly like Jesus Christ, the Elder Brother of the family. It is the invitation to godliness.

Paul makes the mandate clear: "Be imitators of God ... as dearly beloved children, and live a life of love, just as Christ loved us and gave himself up for us as a fragrant offering and sacrifice to God" (Eph. 5:1).

The problem is, some of us mistake godliness for god-like-ness. Like Adam and Eve, we fall prey to the temptation of wanting to "be like God." Then when we get a little spiritual truth under our belts, we start *acting* as if we're omnipotent and omniscient.

True godliness, however, isn't a spiritual trump card that enables us to exalt ourselves over others. It is the quiet, secret, inner longing to become more like Christ, to imitate our Lord and cultivate the fruit of the Spirit. In Philippians 2, Paul exhorts us to "have the same atti-tude as Christ Jesus"—an atti-tude not of spiritual superiority, but of humility, of servanthood, of sacrifice, of love.

If Jesus Christ was, as the Bible claims, the earthly incarna-tion of the Divine Nature, his life and ministry should give us an example to emulate. And what an example it is!

Jesus loved. He reached out to those on the fringes of accept-able society. He fraternized with outcasts, embraced lepers, fed the hungry, offered hope to the despairing. He healed the sick, gave sight to the blind, set the captives free. He lived in grace, in forgiveness, in integrity.

This is the ancestral portrait. This is our spiritual gene pool.

Humility

There must be feelings of humility,
not from nature, but from penitence,
not to rest in them, but to go on to greatness.

—Pascal, 1670

By now it's become a classic—that funny, tearful moment at the Academy Awards when Sally field took the stage to accept her Oscar for *Places in the Heart*. She shook her head, lifted the statue, and said in a voice filled with wonder, "You like me! You really like me!"

Amazing, that this gifted woman, who had spearheaded so many fine films, could still be overwhelmed by the idea that others appreciated and valued her work. It was a glimpse of humility uncharacteristic among the Hollywood elite, and thus especially endearing.

Humility is a virtue often undervalued by the world in which we live. We are taught that we have to look out for Number One, to win through intimidation, to climb the ladder of success no matter who we have to step on in the process. We are encouraged to be our own best friend, to serve as our own public relations agent, to blow our own horn because nobody else will.

God, however, seems to have a different perspective on self-aggrandizement.

Jesus approached the subject with a parable: When somebody invites you to a wedding, he advised, don't take the place of honor. Someone else more distinguished than you might come in, and then you'll be embarrassed when you're asked to move to the cheap seats. Instead, seat yourself among the lowly, and when your host sees you there, he will insist that you move to a place of greater honor. "For everyone who exalts himself will be humbled," Jesus concluded, "and he who humbles himself will be exalted" (Luke 14:7-11).

But we need to be careful to understand what humility is, and what it is not. Humility, Jesus implies in the parable, is knowing the truth about yourself … not pretending to be something you're not. Often pride masks itself as false humility, the kind of worm theology that says, "Woe is me; I am worthless!" Translation: *Look at me; I need attention.*

We are *not* worthless—God in Jesus Christ has rendered us worthy. We can hold our heads up, believe in ourselves, be strong without violating the principles of humility. The key lies in understanding the *source* of our worthiness.

We are worthy because God loves us, loved us even before we accepted that love. We are valued members of God's family because God reached down to us in grace and mercy. We are redeemed, beloved in God's sight, not because of what we have done, but because of what Christ has done on our behalf.

Humor

Pain is deeper than all thought;
laughter is higher than all pain.
— Elbert Hubbard, 1895–1915

In the gripping film *Amistad*, a group of Africans —illegally seized and brought to America by slave traders— mutiny, kill most of their captors, take over the ship, and try to return home. Eventually caught and brought to trial, they watch in wonder and confusion as a group of local Christians gather to pray for them. "It's some sort of dance," one of the Africans suggests as the religious folk get down on their knees.

"It can't be," his friend responds. "They look too miserable to be dancing."

Everyone in the theater laughed. From that point on, the abolitionist Christians who come to lend their support are referred to, from the mutineers' perspective, as "The Miserable Ones."

It's a sad and significant commentary on religious experience. We are The Miserable Ones, the people who have no sense of humor, no joy in life. We don't know how to laugh.

Some Christians might raise an eyebrow at the idea that humor is a spiritual virtue. Mark Twain said "There is no humor in heaven"—I sincerely hope he has found out differently by now. Still, a lot of us Christians seem to think that humor is a sacrilege, that laughter somehow undermines God's public image. Spirituality is serious business, after all.

Abraham's wife Sarah apparently adhered to that perspective. In Genesis 18, when the Lord came to bring her husband the news that she would give birth to a son, Sarah laughed. I'm not sure why she laughed. Maybe she didn't believe it—she was in her nineties, and well past her childbearing years. Or maybe the final fulfillment of the promise was just too wonderful for words. Whatever the reason, when the Lord asked why she had laughed, she denied that she had done so. Obviously, Sarah didn't think laughter was very spiritual.

But God evidently changed her mind. When the long-awaited son finally arrived, she named him Isaac, which means "he laughs"—rather like naming your firstborn after Chuckles the Clown. And she said, "God has brought me laughter, and everyone who hears about this will laugh with me" (Gen. 21:6).

We need to be able to laugh at ourselves, to diffuse stress, to give the gift of lightheartedness to those around us.

And we have plenty of reason to smile. We are recipients of the lavish grace of God; the heavy burden of sin has been lifted from our shoulders. Like the Virtuous Woman in Proverbs 31, we can "laugh at the days to come" because we know our security lies not in ourselves but in our Redeemer.

Integrity

*Whatever games are played with us,
we must play no games with ourselves,
but deal in our privacy with the last honesty and truth.*

— Emerson, 1860

And the winner in the category of Most Absurd Television Commercial Ever Conceived: *"I'm not a doctor, but I play one on TV."* This sterling recommendation is supposed to get viewers to take the word of the handsome, distinguished, white-haired actor when he declares the miraculous healing properties of his product. After all, he plays a doctor on television; surely he knows all about medicine.

Go ahead, laugh. I did. But the scenario is not quite so amusing when we apply it to ourselves: *I'm not a counselor, but I play one when I give advice to my friends and acquaintances. I'm not God, but I play at being omniscient when it comes to other people's problems. I'm not a Christian, but I play one on Sundays.*

Children call this game of pretense "play like," and for a child it can be a healthy stimulation of the imagination. But when adults "play like," God calls it something else. Hypocrisy. Deception. Lack of integrity.

The root of the word "integrity" is the Latin *integer*, meaning one, whole, entire, undivided. From that root we get words like *integrate*, to make one.

And *integrity*, the state of truly being on the inside what we seem to be on the outside.

"May integrity and uprightness protect me," the Psalmist prays, "because my hope is in you" (Ps. 25:21). And indeed, integrity does protect us. Integrity shields us from the exhausting, nerve-wracking practice of trying to put up a front, to convince others that we are something else, something they want or expect us to be.

There is liberty in integrity. No longer do we have to be perfect, to do everything right, to be little gods on shaky pedestals. We can be ourselves—human, flawed, fallible people, ever striving toward greater spiritual understanding.

But before we can take down the fronts with others, we must first learn to be honest with ourselves—and with God. To be people of integrity, we have to face our inadequacies and limitations candidly, give ourselves permission not to be perfect.

God knows we're not perfect. We know it, too, if we can only admit it. We are no less spiritual for owning up to our faults and weaknesses—in fact, God honors such frankness. In the admission of our weaknesses, the power of Christ has opportunity to work.

God calls us to be people of integrity—to be one, entire, whole. To allow the truth of what is inside to be revealed outwardly. For then we can place our trust in God rather than in the appearance of spiritual maturity.

And rather than being a spokesperson for a product we know nothing about, we can speak the truth because we have lived it.

bedience

It is right that what is just should be obeyed.
~ Pascal, 1670

The child, a boy of perhaps five, stood rigid and unyielding as his mother tried to correct him. He had been misbehaving, kicking up a ruckus in the middle of a nice restaurant, disturbing other patrons and generally making a nuisance of himself. The mother took him by the elbow and whispered, "Sit down and behave yourself, young man."

The little boy sat down, crossed his arms, and glared at her. "I may be sittin' down on the outside," he muttered, "but I'm still standin' up on the inside."

External restraint does not necessarily reflect internal obedience. We can do all the right things: stand at attention, salute like little spiritual soldiers, form a straight line heading for heaven's gates. But the Lord is interested in something a little less obvious. God wants not just our submission, but our hearts.

"Blessed are they who keep his statutes," Psalm 119:2 says, "and seek him with all their

30

hearts." Keeping God's statutes is important, to be sure. But the motivation behind that obedience is the key to true godliness.

Why do we obey? Is it because we fear reprisal? Is it because we are concerned about our reputation? Because we are trying to live up to the expectations of others?

Biblical obedience is not a matter of outward appearance but of inward reality. If we obey God out of a spirit of defiance, still "standing up on the inside," our obedience means nothing. "The multitude of your sacrifices—what are they to me?" God says. "Stop bringing meaningless offerings. They have become a burden to me; I am weary of bearing them" (Isa. 1:11, 13-14).

What God wants from us is not just the outward semblance of obedience, but a heart softened to the Divine will. A spirit that acknowledges that God not only has the *right* to our obedience, but knows what is best for us and so can be trusted to lead us.

Obedience in the inner soul is based not on fear but on love. Because we love God, we seek to obey. Because we know God loves us, we can trust that what the Lord asks of us will not be too difficult for us, and will result in our good.

The secular world often mocks what it calls "blind obedience" in religious people. But obedience is not blind. Even when it cannot understand God's reasons, it trusts God's character. Obedience sees with the heart that God is good, and thus submits itself to One who is wiser, stronger, and more faithful.

Passion

When I was a child, my father taught me an important lesson about having passion for life. "Never make major life decisions based solely on money," he said. "Do what you love, and love what you do."

Sad to say, we live in a society that doesn't value passion as my father did. The majority of people drag themselves to work every day, hating what they do but needing to hang onto the security of the paycheck. They lead, as Thoreau observed, "lives of quiet desperation," resigned to a routine existence, finding little joy even in the company of the people they love most.

As Christians, however, our perspective on the ordinariness of life is radically altered by the cross, and by our participation in the work of God. "Whatever you do," Paul says, "work at it with all your heart, as working for the Lord.... It is the Lord Christ you are serving" (Col. 3:23-24).

We are called to be people of passion—people on fire with love for God and for one another. And that passion, that enthusiasm, infuses our world, our work, and our relationships with divine energy.

Christlike passion views everything in our lives—every action, every interaction—through the lens of God's love and grace. The smallest act of love takes on eternal significance; the greatest opportunity leaves us humbled and breathless in the presence of the Spirit's power.

My father's advice to me is good counsel for all who would serve God wholeheartedly: Follow your passion.

Do you have a heart for children? Use it to defend the defenseless, to teach, to protect the young from abuse and neglect.

Does your soul weep for the homeless, the hungry, the outcast? Use your energy to work for change, to show compassion, to feed and shelter and touch those who need to see Jesus through human love.

Ministry is not just for the preachers, the seminarians, the ordained. The Spirit calls all of us to reconcile the world to God, to give ourselves in an outpouring of redemptive love. It doesn't matter if you're a doctor, a plumber, a teacher, or a stay-at-home mom—all of us can embrace the call of God with zeal and joy.

Follow your passion. It will lead you to your heart's true home.

Perseverance

Perseverance is more prevailing than violence; and many things which cannot be overcome when they are together, yield themselves up when taken little by little.

~ Plutarch, 2nd c. A.D.

In the blockbuster hit *Titanic*, Rose—a young woman trapped in a social structure she despises and engaged to an abusive, power-driven man—stands on the ledge of the great ocean liner about to commit suicide. She has no hope, no way out. Then Jack Dawson, a penniless artist, talks her back from the edge. She slips and falls. He grabs her hand and promises, "I won't let go."

Throughout the movie, the theme reasserts itself. Jack refuses to let social convention stand in the way of love. "I won't let go," he repeats as Rose's mother and friends try to keep them apart. As the ship goes down, he holds her close and says once more, "I won't let go." Rose survives, hanging onto a piece of floating debris. And Jack, bobbing in the frigid water at her side, dies still holding her hand.

He was true to his promise. Even in death, he didn't let go.

It's a picture of the power of perseverance. The kind of perseverance that holds on, in the face of insurmountable odds, to faith and hope, to the belief that life is worth living, and—for the Christian—to the conviction that God "won't let go."

The writer of Hebrews gives an extraordinary illustration of perseverance. Hebrews 11 cites examples of the great warriors of the faith, those who "kept the Passover, passed through the Red Sea, brought down the walls of Jericho... and received back their dead, raised to life again" (Heb. 11:28-35, NIV).

But the catalogue of saints and heroes in Hebrews 11 doesn't stop with the victors. For it's not success that demonstrates the presence and power of God, but perseverance. There were "others," who were stoned, sawed in two, put to death by the sword. "These were commended for their faith, yet none of them received what had been promised" (Heb. 11:39).

We prefer the heroic stories that have a happy ending, that resolve victoriously. But real life doesn't always give us a conquest. We may never live to see the fulfillment of some of the promises, yet the promises are true, and our perseverance is not in vain.

And so we determine, in God's name, that we "won't let go." We hold onto our faith when days are dark and we can't see the way ahead. We latch onto hope when there is no light at the end of the tunnel. We wait, when we have no direction. Sometimes our perseverance seems like a frantic grasping at the debris around us, trying to find something to buoy us up in the deep, cold water. It would be easy to let go, to give up.

But we hold on. Because even in the dark night of the soul, God is present, reaching out to us, promising, "I won't let go."

Purity

The Boy In the Plastic Bubble is the story of a young man who, because of a rare disorder in his immune system, is forced to live his entire life cut off from the world. His plastic bubble, a sanitized space free from germs, protects him. He can never touch anyone or even get close to anyone, because the ordinary viruses that we live with every day would ravage his body and cause his death. He is protected, certainly. But he is also imprisoned.

When religious people begin to talk about purity, they sometimes leave their listeners with the impression that the Lord's followers are *The Christians In the Plastic Bubble*. Wanting to keep ourselves pure, unstained and uninfluenced by the world, we cut ourselves off, fearing contact with those "on the outside." We hire plumbers and carpenters and printers from the Christian yellow pages. We send our kids to Christian schools or teach them at home. We socialize exclusively with other Christians. We drive Christian cars, eat Christian pizza,

watch Christian television, listen to Christian radio, play the Christian version of Trivial Pursuit.

But purity, according to biblical standards, is not based on externals. Jesus claims, contrary to Jewish tradition, that it is not what goes *into* people that defiles them, but what comes *out of* them (Matt. 15:17-19). Paul teaches that nothing God has created is, in and of itself, unclean (Rom. 14:14). And the letter to Titus gives a clear picture of the internal nature of true purity: "To the pure, all things are pure, but to those who are corrupted and do not believe, nothing is pure" (Titus 1:15).

Why are we so afraid of contaminating ourselves? Jesus wasn't. He rubbed shoulders with the sinful masses, welcomed lepers, had dinner parties with prostitutes and tax collectors, ate with "unclean hands."

The plastic bubble may safeguard us, but it also confines us. Purity doesn't need isolation for protection. We don't purify our minds and souls by imprisoning ourselves in a bubble of righteousness and refusing to be desecrated by the world around us.

Love makes us pure.

Love creates in us a tenderheartedness, a habit of Christlikeness, a willingness to risk. Love gives us the vision to see Jesus in those around us, and the compassion to get involved. Love frees us from the fear of spiritual infection and strengthens our soul's immune system.

Reach out to those around you.

Jesus is the only fortress you will ever need.

Repentance

ike a spider dangling over the pit of hell by a single thread...."

Jonathan Edwards' simile is, without question, one of the most memorable images ever devised to convey the necessity of repentance. That sermon, "Sinners in the Hands of an Angry God" may have been a scare tactic, what modern folks would call "fire-and-brimstone preaching," but it worked. Quite

literally, it put the fear of God into people. And it gave us a metaphor that has endured for more than two hundred years.

In terms of initial salvation, Edwards' illustration is certainly an apt one. We often have to come to the end of our spiritual rope, to the exhaustion of our own resources, before we see the need to repent and turn to the Lord.

But repentance is not simply

a one-time act, a moment of epiphany in which we see the enormity of sin and call out to God for redemption. For the believer, repentance is a state of mind and heart, a willingness to turn—and keep turning—away from anything in our lives that threatens to separate us from the Lord we love and serve.

If repentance means "to turn around, to change your mind, and go in the other direction," then our daily lives are filled with repentance decisions. Choosing to obey rather than resist. Opting to listen rather than tell God what to do. Deciding to forgive rather than seek revenge. Determining to love rather than nurture resentment. "In repentance and rest is your salvation," the Lord reminds us. "In quietness and trust is your strength" (Isa. 30:15, NIV).

We need repentance of sin for salvation. But we also need repentance of "self." We need to have hearts tuned to hear the voice of God's Spirit within. We need to hear that still small voice that tells us to turn around and go the other direction.

We need a change of mind.

In the world's view, changing your mind is a sign of instability, of vacillation. Once you make a decision, you stand by it. You stick to your guns. You dig your heels in and refuse to be moved.

But God wants to move us, to change us, to conform us to the image of Jesus Christ. And repentance is the first step in that change.

So let your heart reach toward God in repentance.

It's okay to change your mind.

Reverence

*God prefers bad verses recited with a pure heart,
to the finest verses possible chanted by the wicked.*

~ Voltaire, 1764

In a quiet sanctuary illuminated by the soft glow from stained-glass windows, people kneel in silence, praying, meditating. Nuns, perhaps, or priests or monks or pastors. Holy people. People set apart for service to God.

It's an image of reverence that pervades religious consciousness. But there was another kind of monk—one who discovered a deep relationship with God amid the clattering of dishes in a monastery kitchen. His name was Brother Lawrence, and his little book, *The Practice of the Presence of God*, gives us a different perspective of reverence. "Lord of all pots and pans and things," he prayed, "make me a saint by getting meals and washing up the plates!" Now, here is an image of reverence we can identify with.

Most of us, after all, have to discover God in the midst of a harried, busy schedule. We rarely find time for meditation, and when we do we're often so exhausted that we fall asleep at our prayers. We don't have the luxury—or the discipline, perhaps—of hours of uninterrupted solitude with God.

But reverence is more a state of the heart than a matter of silence. We revel in those times of quiet meditation, certainly. We long for them, and welcome them when they come. But we can, like Brother Lawrence, learn to give ourselves to a spirit of reverence no matter what we're doing.

The prophet Jeremiah reminds us of our motivation for approaching God with reverence: "No one is like you, O Lord; you are great, and your name is mighty in power. Who should not revere you, O King of the nations? There is no one like you" (Jer. 10:7).

And that truth is all we need to live in a spirit of awe and worship before the Lord. After all, Moses was herding sheep in the wilderness when God appeared in the burning bush. Ruth was trying to console her grieving mother-in-law when God stepped in to change her life forever. Mary the mother of Christ was going about her daily work when the angel announced that she would bear the Messiah. To each of them, God revealed that "there is no one like the Lord."

No matter where we are, no matter what we're doing, we can live in a state of reverence toward God.

O Lord, make me a saint by driving the car pool and looking after the kids.

Make me a saint by cooperating with my boss and co-workers.

Make me a saint by doing laundry and loading the dishwasher.

Let me hear your voice above the clamor of my daily life, for "there is no one like you."

Self-Acceptance

It is difficult to make a man miserable while he feels worthy of himself and claims kindred to the great God who made him.

—Abraham Lincoln, 1862

For years the nation watched as the tabloids chronicled one of the world's most famous women in her private—yet very public—Battle of the Bulge. Oprah Winfrey, the uncontested queen of daytime talk-shows, is a beautiful, talented woman. But for years she struggled, on camera and off, to recreate herself. She lost weight, dropping down to a svelte size six. But then she gained it again, in the yo-yo syndrome so familiar to anyone who has ever tried to slim down. Every pound was publicly scrutinized, criticized, discussed.

Then Oprah made a decision. She got on a healthy eating program and exercise regimen. She stabilized at 150 pounds or so. And she made a public declaration: "I am finally comfortable with myself," she said. "I don't need to be a size 6. I can be a happy and successful 12 or 14."

Self-acceptance is a virtue often challenged by the religious community. Suspicious of pop psychology and self-help programs, they claim that self-acceptance is not nearly as important to the Christian's life as God's acceptance. What really matters, they say, is what God thinks of me; never mind what I think of myself.

To some extent, they may be right. God's acceptance of us in Christ Jesus is the fundamental truth upon which we build our lives. But if we ignore the necessity of self-acceptance, we render ourselves unable to take full advantage of the abundant life offered to us in our Redeemer.

Paul gives this exhortation to Christians: "For by the grace given me I say to every one of you. Do not think of yourselves more highly than you ought, but rather think of yourself with sober judgment, in accordance with the measure of faith God has given you" (Rom. 12:3).

Yes, we need to acknowledge our limitations, to face our weaknesses, to confess our sins. But if we want to be active, productive participants in the realm of God, we also need to recognize our gifts, to appreciate our strengths, to build on the abilities God has given us. We need to balance humility with confidence.

Flannery O'Connor, a brilliant writer and devout believer, was once asked why she became a writer. "Because I'm good at it," she replied. It was a statement of fact, not a declaration of arrogance. Self-acceptance is not pride. It is the proportional, "sober judgment" that allows us to see ourselves as we truly are, as God sees us.

Almighty God created us, redeemed us, called us, endowed us with gifts and abilities and perceptions. To demean the gift is to insult the Giver.

Self-Awareness

Remember the classic children's story, *The Secret Garden?* Hidden behind high walls and a locked gate, the garden is neglected, overgrown, and dying. But when Mary, an orphaned girl, discovers the key and opens the gate, miraculous things begin to happen. She enlists the help of her friend Dickon and her cousin Colin. They clear away the undergrowth, nurture the budding plants, and watch in wonder as the garden blooms back to life. Colin, a spoiled, sickly, rich boy, finds healing and hope in the miracle. Mary herself discovers friendship, love, a new family, and a new life.

Most of us have a secret garden inside, a neglected, walled-off part of our souls. Maybe we've just spent too much of our time and energy making a living, raising children, caring for infirm parents, or acquiring the external trappings of the good life. Maybe we're a little afraid to put the key in the lock and find out what's inside. Self-examination can be a risky business.

But God vastly more makes it very clear that the important stuff is inside of us, not on the outside. "The word," Deuteronomy 30:14 tells us, "is very near you; it is in your mouth and in your heart so you may obey it." Jesus said, "The kingdom of God is within you" (Luke 17:21).

We might expect Christ's words to be addressed to the disciples, those who already believed and followed faithfully. Yet he was speaking to the Pharisees—those religious leaders who were convinced that access to the kingdom of God lay in adherence to a multitude of regulations and laws. "Look to your heart," Jesus was saying, "not to your rules."

But we're suspicious of our hearts. It's easier to follow a list of regulations than to listen for the still small voice inside. It's comfortable to keep to the well-worn paths, rather than take the risk of opening the secret garden and cutting away the dead branches.

Self-awareness is a scary prospect. We are likely to find dark places in our innermost souls, areas of undergrowth where the sunlight of God's renewing love has never penetrated. We may dig up hidden motivations we don't want to admit, shadowed corners of selfishness and greed, tangled branches of deceit. Secrets we'd like to keep locked away. But we'll also uncover fragrant roses about to bud, long-buried bulbs pushing their blooms toward the light.

The Lord already knows the state of our inner garden. There is no risk of losing God's love. The transformation may be painful at first, but the miracle is worth it.

Self-Discipline

Do not consider painful what is good for you.
—Euripides, 431 b.c.

In the movie, *G.I. Jane*, Demi Moore plays the role of a woman determined to become the first female certified as a Navy Seal. The discipline is relentless—long hours of rigorous physical training, mental and emotional conditioning, and wartime simulation. Her superiors, unwilling to accept a woman as part of their elite corps, are certain she'll never make the cut, and they do everything they can to discourage her.

But what fascinated me about the movie was the obvious training Demi Moore had imposed upon herself in preparation for the role. One scene shows her doing one-armed push-ups—clearly the actress herself, not a stunt double. She grunts with exertion, and her well-developed biceps bulge. It's evident she's been busy off-camera even before the first frame was shot. The grueling torture the character endures could easily have been rendered through Hollywood's sleight-of-hand, but Demi Moore's own self-discipline was very real.

Self-discipline is a private, secret virtue. It's not a practice that brings us external rewards, the accolades of others, or public recognition. And, to tell the truth, it's not the kind of virtue that most of us get a lot of pleasure out of pursuing.

But it is worth it. Sweating it out behind the cameras may not be glamorous, but it brings reality to what we do when the lights come up and the action begins.

Each of us has an individual calling to self-discipline. It may be the habit of setting aside regular time for prayer and Bible study. It may be curtailing the tendency toward workaholism in order to spend more time with the family. It may mean living on a budget, or finding the energy to do volunteer work, or tithing, or the rigorous commencement of a healthy diet and exercise program.

And we might as well admit it, self-discipline doesn't come easy. Hebrews 12:11 gives us a realistic picture: "No discipline seems pleasant at the time, but painful. Later on, however, it produces a harvest of righteousness and peace for those who have been trained by it."

Self-discipline is personal training—training in spiritual growth, in physical strength and health, in mental awareness. Like Demi Moore pumping up for her role, we work through the pain, through the discomfort and inconvenience, with our eyes fixed on the goal.

And we need to remember that our call to self-discipline is just that: our call. God may challenge others to a different kind of discipline, one we do not understand or cannot recognize.

Whatever God is asking you to do, whatever self-discipline is required, take a little advice from the athletes: *Just do it*. The rewards will be greater than the cost.

Sincerity

During the Italian Renaissance, when the art of sculpture reached its golden age, it became a practice among inferior artists to "wax" their works. A thin layer of clear wax smoothed across the marble disguised the minute pits, cracks, and imperfections and gave the appearance of an undamaged surface. The finest sculptors, however, created their models without resorting to the deception of wax. That flawless satiny finish of the polished marble on a Michelangelo *Pieta* or *David* was, in Latin, *sine cera*—without wax—and from that image we derive the English word, *sincerity*. What you see is what you get.

We live in a society where sincerity is almost as rare as a Michelangelo masterpiece. Everything seems to be "waxed": advertisers make false claims about their products; car companies repair wrecked vehicles and sell them as new; "satisfied customers" tout the benefits of plastic surgery, anti-aging remedies, and surgical hair replacement techniques. The credo of the twentieth century is *caveat emptor*—let the buyer beware.

You'd think in this well-waxed world, Christianity would stand out as the exception. Surely in the realm of faith, what you see is what you get. Christians wouldn't gloss over the surface to give the impression of flawlessness—would we?

Well, don't we? We say, either directly or by implication, "Come to Jesus and all your problems will be solved," when that's not what Jesus promised at all. We allow others to interpret that the "abundant life" necessarily includes material abundance, or at the very least freedom from financial or emotional struggle.

But Christ, the reflection of Divine Perfection, doesn't need our human attempts at making faith appear more attractive. God values sincerity—the unwaxed, unvarnished truth of who we are. As James 3:17 reminds us, "The wisdom that comes from heaven is first of all pure; then peace loving, considerate, submissive, full of mercy and good fruit, impartial and sincere."

And the world, too, is looking for that kind of veracity. People are drawn not to perfection, but to reality. They need to witness—from us, with all our faults and failings—how God's power can work in real people whose conflicts and adversities mirror their own. They need to know, because they see it in us, that our Lord is genuinely compassionate, truly gracious, authentically loving.

With all its struggles and difficulties, faith is a masterpiece, a finely-sculpted testimony to the majesty of the Creator. No camouflage is needed, no apologies required. We don't have to put on a wax job to make the Lord look good. All we need is sincerity.

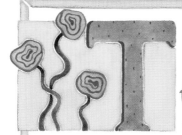

Teachableness

Oh, would that my mind could let fall its dead ideas as the tree does its withered leaves!
—Andre Gide, 1947

A small congregation was facing some difficult decisions. Its denomination was moving in a new direction, and the members of the church were apprehensive about what those changes might mean for them. "Let's pray about it," the pastor urged. "Let's meet once a week and seek God's direction."

But to the pastor's dismay, only one person showed up for the prayer meetings—the president of the congregation. "We don't want to pray about it," the president stated flatly. "We already know what we think about these new developments, and if we pray, there's a chance that God might change our minds."

It sounds shocking, but don't we often take a similar stance with God? We get our minds made up about what the Lord means and fail to listen—really listen—to what the Spriit is saying about our situation. Our prayers become sealed letters rather than open dialogues, and we cut ourselves off from the remote possibility that God may have something else in mind. We are sure—so very sure—that we know the mind of Christ. We stop seeking and settle into a routine of confirming what we already know.

But Jesus valued the teachable heart. "Unless you change and become like little children, you will never enter the kingdom of heaven" (Matt. 18:3).

Children eagerly absorb all that is taught to them. Like sponges, they soak up language, behavioral patterns, moral precepts, manners, and truth. They accept challenges with enthusiasm. They try on unfamiliar ideas. They grow.

The teachable soul responds to God's voice not with resistance, but with openness. If we're teachable, we will put aside our preconceived notions and consider the possibility that God just might be taking us in new directions. We will pray with a listening heart, ready to respond to the Holy Spirit's nudgings within us. We will keep an open mind when we read the Scriptures instead of assuming we already understand what the Word means. We will listen with respectfulness to those who believe differently and try to see truth from their perspective.

And when we do, something wonderful happens. The burden of always being right is lifted from our shoulders, and we experience a freedom in our spiritual lives that we never imagined. No longer do we need to defend God's truth or convince others of the accuracy of our personal perspectives.

God is quite capable of leading others in the way they need to go. Our responsibility is to listen for ourselves, to be teachable—like little children.

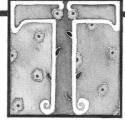

Thankfulness

A grateful mind
By owing, owes not, but still pays,
at once indebted and discharged.

— John Milton, 1667

Thanksgiving: A national holiday that occurs late in November, ostensibly set aside to recall our many blessings and give thanks to God. More often, in the last decade of the twentieth century, referred to as "Turkey Day"—traditionally marked by overindulgence in food and drink, overexposure to television football, and ten hours of uncomfortable and superficial interaction with relatives we try to avoid the rest of the year.

Whatever happened to thankfulness?

When did we lose track of the importance of ongoing "thanksgiving"—not just a cursory nod toward the Giver of all good gifts during a hasty blessing over the turkey, but a deep spirit of gratitude, a true awareness of the blessedness of our lives?

Of all the inner virtues important to the development of Christlikeness, I believe that thankfulness is one of the most neglected and underrated. *Of course I'm thankful—I say grace over my meals, don't I? I give my tithe, attend church, sing "God is so good."*

But how often am I simply overwhelmed by my blessings when I stand in the shower and have an unlimited supply of hot, clean water to wash with? Do I get teary-eyed with gratitude when I'm held in the arms of my beloved? Does my heart well up with thankfulness at the sight of my friends and family gathered around the dinner table?

Thankfulness has little to do with how much we own. A heart of gratitude is based, instead, on an understanding of the source of our spiritual and emotional riches. "Enter into [God's] gates with thanksgiving," the Psalmist says, "and into his courts with praise; give thanks to him and praise his name. For the Lord is good and his love endures for ever; his faithfulness continues through all generations" (Ps. 100:4-5).

All we require, in order to cultivate a grateful heart, is a little bit of time. Time to reflect on the outpouring of Christ's love that is evident in our lives. Time to consider what our existence might be like apart from the grace and mercy and direction of Almighty God. Time to remind ourselves what really matters. Time to look into the eyes of those we love and see our Savior's generosity reflected there.

Thanksgiving is not a holiday—it is a holy way of life. It is a new perspective that guards us from greed and self-centeredness, that tenderizes our hearts and renews our minds.

Every day is Thanksgiving to those who know God's spiritual bounty.

Tolerance

In necessary things, unity; in doubtful things, liberty; in all things, charity.
— Richard Baxter, 1615/1691

Her name was Jackie. She was an attractive young woman, gifted in both athletics and academics. She stood out in our high school—but not because she was bright, or friendly, or intelligent, or the best spiker on the volleyball team. She stood out because she was black. People burned crosses in her front yard, threw eggs at her house, called her names, tried to intimidate her into giving up and going back "where she belonged." It was a turbulent time, a heartbreaking era. I couldn't understand then, any more than I can understand now, why my friend Jackie would bear the brunt of cruelty, injustice, even violence, just because her skin was not white.

But the twentieth century has no monopoly on intolerance. Nero, Attila, Caesar, Hitler—as far back as history stretches, civilizations have systematically waged war, oppressed the underdog, and annihilated entire cultures in order to maintain their power and control.

To our shame, the church is not immune: the Crusades, the Inquisition, slavery, and anti-Semitism all testify to the appalling effects of intolerance. In Jesus' day, the Pharisees tried to undermine his ministry, and even the disciples who followed him and listened to his teachings were not tolerant of everything he did. They reprimanded him for talking to a Samaritan woman, and tried to keep children from bothering him in the town square. They pushed aside the lame and the beggars and the prostitutes and the tax collectors—the very people Christ had come to save.

Jesus, however, both preached and modeled tolerance. "Whoever is not against you is for you," he reminded the disciples (Luke 9:50). The Messiah was an advocate for the poor, the homeless, the sick, the imprisoned, the outcasts of the world. Most of his earthly ministry was spent reaching out to people we probably wouldn't be comfortable welcoming into our churches.

Yet if we want to be imitators of Christ, we need to cultivate the virtue of tolerance. And tolerance is not merely political correctness or public forbearance, pasting on a false smile. It is an attitude of the heart, a recognition that all people, whether they are "like us" or not, are made in the image of God, precious in his sight, and worthy of honor.

Tolerance does not mean that we necessarily agree with what another person does or believes. It means that we give people space to come to faith in their own way, recognizing that God alone discerns the heart. It means that we approach those around us with love rather than with judgment.

We are not called to change people, to force them to see the light. We are not called to re-create others in our own image.

We are called to love.

Wisdom

It's one of those bizarre stories in Scripture—two women, laying claim to the same infant child, come to King Solomon for a judgment. "Three days after I gave birth," the first says, "this woman who lives in the same house had her child. Her baby died, and during the middle of the night she got up and switched babies with me." The second woman denies the story, saying that the living baby is hers.

Quite a dilemma for Solomon. And even more bizarre than the quandary is the King's solution: cut the baby in half and give half a child to each mother. The real mother, of course, cannot bear to see her infant son die, so she pleads, "Give the living baby to her! Don't let him die." And Solomon, realizing that no true mother would sacrifice her baby's life to prove a point, has his answer (1 Kings 3:16-28).

Solomon, the Bible tells us, was the wisest man who ever

lived. Early in his reign as King of Israel, God came to him in a dream and made him an offer he couldn't refuse: "Ask for whatever you want me to give you."

Solomon asked not for wealth or honor, but for wisdom. "Give your servant a discerning heart to govern your people, and to distinguish between right and wrong." God was pleased with the request, and gave Solomon wisdom that set him apart from all others—and great wealth and power in the bargain (1 Kings 3: 5-13).

Solomon obviously realized something we often forget: Knowledge can be cultivated through study; power can be gained by conquest; honor can be acquired by deeds of greatness. But wisdom is a gift from God. Anyone who lacks wisdom, James 1:5 reminds us, should ask God, who "gives generously to all without finding fault."

Perhaps the key to Solomon's wisdom lay in his awareness that he needed it. Too often we depend upon ourselves—our instincts, our training, our education, our reputation—rather than looking to God for wisdom. But being wise doesn't mean knowing everything, memorizing large portions of Scripture, or having a list of degrees after your name. It means being able to see situations from God's point of view— and having the capacity to discern our own limitations.

What do we get when we ask for wisdom? Most of the time, we get questions—lots of them. Hard questions. Many more questions than answers.

But the questions drive us back to God. And dependence upon the Almighty is the ultimate wisdom.

The
Public
Virtues

Acceptance

If we cannot end our differences, at least we can make the world safe for diversity.

—John F. Kennedy, 1963

few months ago I watched a television program entitled "Difficult Daughters." It wasn't about daughters, really, but about the tenuous and sometimes painful relationships between mothers and daughters—it might, in fact, have been called "Difficult Mothers." Some of the mothers, according to the expert, abandoned their daughters too soon, resulting in the young woman's fierce independence and outright rebellion. Others held on too long, never severing the apron strings and producing offspring who were utterly dependent, incapable of making decisions for themselves. One mother bewailed, "If only my daughter were different."

Finally the host cut to the heart of the matter. "You have to *accept*," she said. "Accept the fact that your daughter *is* different— different from you. Accept the reality that life doesn't always go the way we'd like. Accept what is, and move on from there."

It's wise advice for us Christians, whether we have problem children or not. Life doesn't always deal us the perfect hand. If we want to have peace in our lives, we need to begin with acceptance.

The apostle Paul gives a clear picture of what that acceptance entails. "I have learned to be content whatever the circumstances. I know what it is to be in need, and I know what it is to have plenty. I have learned the secret of being content in any and every situation, whether well fed or hungry, whether living in plenty or in want. I can do everything through him who gives me strength" (Phil. 4:11-13).

Acceptance is a matter of trust. Trust not in ourselves, or in our ability to convert those around us to our way of perceiving things, but trust in God, who alone can see the heart. There are things in our lives that we *can* change, of course. If we're physically and mentally able, we can work instead of remaining idle and expecting someone else to pay the bills. We can take steps to improve the quality of our lives. We can spend more time with our families and set aside opportunities to get to know God better.

But we can't change other people. Anyone who's ever been married or had children knows the futility of trying to shape another human being into the image of what they "should be." That's God's job, and we need to leave it in the Lord's capable hands.

The heart that accepts is a heart at peace. Rather than constantly striving to re-create our lives and the people we love, let's take a lesson from Paul. Whatever state we're in, we can learn to be content through the grace given to us in Jesus Christ.

The well-known prayer of Reinhold Niebuhr reminds us: Serenity accepts the things we cannot change. Courage changes the things we can.

May God grant us wisdom to know the difference.

Compassion

*Endow the living with the Tears
You squander on the Dead.*
— Emily Dickinson, 1862

The story is told of an old Hasidic rabbi who shared his wisdom with a young rabbinical student. Overcome by the rich treasure of his mentor's teachings, the young man cried out, "I love you, my Master!"

The old man thought about this for a moment and then turned to the student with a sad expression on his face. "How can you claim to love me," he responded, "when you do not know what makes me weep?"

In Christian circles we talk a lot about compassion — empathizing with others, developing sensitivity to the struggles of those less fortunate than ourselves, ministering to the needy. But God requires more of us than random acts of charity. God calls us to "love our neighbor as ourselves."

It's a monumental challenge. We know what makes us weep. But do we know the hidden anguish in the hearts of those around us? Do we get close enough to see the source of other people's tears? Even more importantly, do we know what makes God weep?

The Gospel of Matthew gives us a clue. "When [Jesus] saw the crowds, he had compassion upon them, because they were harassed and helpless, like sheep without a shepherd" (Matt. 9:36).

The human condition has changed little in two thousand years. People today, even members of our families and churches, citizens of our own hometowns—our literal neighbors—are harassed and helpless, wandering sheep. But it's not enough simply to herd them into church and tell them spiritual stories about the Good Shepherd. Jesus did more than teach them. He lived among the lost sheep, healing them and feeding them, listening to their stories of brokenness and despair, of shattered dreams, of unfulfilled longings and unmet needs.

A lot of shepherdless sheep roam among us. They are waiting—the harassed, the helpless, the aimless, the defenseless. We can bring hope and healing, direction and protection. But we dare not go to them with superficial piety. We must go as Jesus did.

He loved them. He knew what made them weep. And he wept with them.

Constancy

Behind the dim unknown, standeth God within the shadow, keeping watch above his own.
— James Russell Lowell, 1844

As a child, I was fascinated with the heavens. My dad had a telescope, and he would let me look through it at the night sky. He didn't know much about astronomy, I realize now, but he knew enough to convey to his daughter a sense of wonder at the immensity and constancy of God's creation.

"See the Big Dipper?" he said, pointing. "OK, now follow from there—that's the North Star. Back in the old days,

before compasses and radar, sailors navigated by that star."

I didn't understand. If you were on the other side of the world, wouldn't that star be in a different place? But no, Daddy said, it was always there, indicating North. The Polestar.

It was a constant, like the sun coming up in the east or Venus rising at dusk. A fixed marker in an ever-spinning world.

That was forty years ago. The universe spins faster today, it seems, re-creating itself at a mind-boggling rate. Everything is up for grabs; what was true last night is false this morning. Check your e-mail: New revelations are speeding down the information highway at an astonishing clip.

The world needs a little constancy. An anchor. A sure direction.

Paul describes people of faith as the Polestar that keeps the world pointed in the right direction: "Blameless and pure, children of God without fault in a crooked and depraved generation … you shine like stars in the universe as you hold out the word of life" (Phil. 2:15-16).

What does it mean to be the North Star for the spiritual universe? It means holding fast to the truth of God's mercy and grace. It means being faithful to God and to others. It means founding our lives, our relationships, and our actions on the bedrock of Christ's sacrificial love.

All around us, people are cut off from their moorings, adrift on a sea of uncertainty. Any port can look like home to a sinking ship. Perhaps it's time to set aside our negative theologies, our pet doctrines, the differences that divide us from the rest of God's people, and let one constant truth illuminate like a beacon: God's love endures forever.

Welcome the travelers. Hold out the Word of Life.

Love is the Polestar that draws people home to God, the never-changing mark that guides them into a safe harbor.

Dedication

> When we do the best that we can,
> we never know what miracle is wrought in our life,
> or in the life of another.
> — Helen Keller, 1913

It's one of those tales that often gets lost in planning Bible studies. Not a glamorous story, or a particularly dramatic one. No big fish swallowing up the prophet, or lions threatening to eat God's people. Just a simple story of dedication in the face of great odds.

Jerusalem had been conquered, its walls destroyed, its people carried off into slavery. One of those people, a prophet named Nehemiah, was serving as cupbearer to King Artaxerxes when the call of God came to him: *Go and rebuild the walls of Jerusalem.*

With the King's approval, Nehemiah went to Jerusalem, only to find himself faced with a daunting challenge. The city lay in ruins, the gates burned. Only a handful of Jews still remained in the great City of God.

This was Nehemiah's call, but it obviously wasn't a job Nehemiah could do alone. He needed help. And so the priests of God — the few who were left — gathered around to share his dream. Each one, the Bible tells us, "made repairs in front of his own house" (Neh. 3:29). As opposition increased, they eventually had to work with a sword in one hand and a trowel in the other. But the job got done. The wall was rebuilt, the gates restored, because each worker committed to the space in front of his own house.

It's easier, sometimes, for us as Christians to proclaim our dedication to the larger work of God—to the salvation of nations, to evangelistic outreach in far-off places. But real dedication to the Lord's purposes often means getting dirty in the ditches that border our own homes.

It's not a glamorous call, this dedication to the everyday. Serving lunch in a soup kitchen or spending the afternoon in a nursing home doesn't win Nobel prizes. Providing refuge for an abused wife, or offering a day's respite for an AIDS caregiver doesn't hold much in the way of drama or excitement. Dealing with broken relationships in our own families doesn't win us any accolades.

It's just hard work. Mundane work. It's emotional and spiritual bricklaying.

Still, the walls need to be shored up. Relationships need to be healed. The environment needs a good scrubbing. People need the touch of a hand and the light of a friendly face. Children are homeless. Old men are hungry. Single mothers bear the weight of the world on their shoulders.

We are called, like Nehemiah's helpers, to restore the walls in front of our houses.

I'll do mine if you'll do yours. And before we know it, the walls will stand strong again.

Determination

He who is fixed to a star does not change his mind.
— Leonardo da Vinci, c. 1500

In the white, white world of Olympic cross-country skiing, one face stands out. A black face, the smiling countenance of a farmer from a small village in Kenya. His name is Philip Boit. He misses his family, he says, since he spends so much time training in Finland—there is no snow in Africa, after all. He misses his cows.

Philip Boit isn't a very good cross-country skier. He's awkward on the snow, and sometimes falls down. But he gets up again and keeps going.

His Olympic debut was, in objective terms, a disaster. The race was lengthy and arduous, and he crossed the finish line long after the medals had been decided. But he did finish. Other skiers, more experienced than he, simply gave up. Not Philip Boit. He was determined. And with that trademark smile on his face, he vowed to be back in four years when the winter games convened again. He'd be better next time, he promised.

That kind of determination is a virtue we all might do well to emulate. God certainly values it. In Luke 11, Jesus tells his listeners, "Ask and it will be given to you; seek and you will find; knock and the door will be opened to you" (Luke 11:9).

The verbs in the passage imply ongoing action: Ask, and keep on asking. Seek, and keep on seeking. Knock, and keep on knocking.

Do you desire a deeper relationship with God? Go after it the way Philip Boit has sought Olympic glory. Give yourself to the search, heart and mind and soul; keep on asking, seeking, knocking. God will open the door.

Do you want a richer family life? Make it a priority. Don't let your job rule your life. Take a vacation with the kids. Declare Friday night as date night with your spouse—just the two of you, alone.

Do you want to be a better friend to those closest to you? Determine to give yourself more freely—to be honest about your struggles and doubts. Let them share in your joy and sorrow. And make yourself available to support them in triumph and disaster.

Whatever our God-given goals, our dreams, our desires—they will remain inaccessible to us until we determine that we will not give them up without a fight. Nothing easily won is highly valuable. Relationships, education, spiritual and emotional growth—all take time and energy, investment of our very souls. The kind of determination that makes the effort worthwhile even if we don't win the gold.

For if we have determination, we will come back stronger tomorrow. More skilled next week. Further along next month. More ready for the challenge next year.

Ask, and keep on asking. Seek, and keep on seeking. Knock, and keep on knocking. The door opens to the determined heart.

Fairness

Do not measure another's coat on your own body.
— Malay Proverb

"Mommy, it's not fair!" The cry goes out, in nearly every household across the nation, in every courtroom, on the Senate floor, almost every day of the year. Someone gets the short straw, the smaller piece of the corporate pie, the lesser advantage. And whether the subject at hand is sharing toys or dividing up the national budget, the prevailing expectation is that when the smoke clears, things should be fair.

Human beings have a strong, built-in sense of fairness—any four-year old can tell you that. It's not fair for her to get a cookie if I don't get one. It's not fair to let her take my doll away.

The problem is, we often see fairness from only one side—ours. And when the judgment goes against us, we claim unfairness.

Jesus told the story about a landowner who needed laborers to harvest in his vineyard. He went to the marketplace early in the morning and hired the men who were standing around,

agreeing with them up front on a fair day's wages. At noon he went back and hired more. Again at three o'clock. And at five.

When the day's work was over, the laborers lined up to get their pay. The ones who had worked the least were given the agreed-upon wage, so the ones who had worked all day expected more. It was only fair. But when their turn came to be paid, they received the same amount as those who had only worked an hour. "It's not fair!" they complained. "You have made them equal to us who have borne the burden of the work and the heat of the day" (Matt. 20:1-16).

We'd like to think of ourselves as more noble than that, but don't we do the same thing? We see God blessing someone who isn't nearly as "mature" or "spiritual" as we think we are, and we mutter under our breath that it's unfair. We look at other people's behavior and judge the condition of their heart.

If we want to cultivate the virtue of fairness, we need to begin by accepting the truth that only God is capable of seeing the heart and judging rightly. The Lord tells us not to judge, and for good reason. We can only see the outside. We may think we can evaluate another person's spiritual maturity, but we can never know how far that person has come just to get to the place we designate as "immature."

Our responsibility is to look up to God, not down on others. As one old woman put it, "I got enough to handle just keepin' my own front porch swept off."

Fairness doesn't necessarily mean that the cookies are divided evenly. It means that we trust God to do the dividing.

Faithfulness

We trust not because a god exists,
but because this God exists.
— C. S. Lewis, 1955

Amid great controversy in the religious community—including a disclaimer from the Catholic church—the television series *Nothing Sacred* aired on prime time. To my way of thinking, the show was misnamed: it should have been called *Everything Sacred*, for that is the attitude portrayed by the maverick priest Father Ray. In that first episode, Ray finds himself face to face with the woman he loved before he took his vows. When she observes that he has given himself to Christlikeness in pursuing his vocation, Father Ray responds with a statement that shook me to the core: "That's the problem with becoming like Jesus," he says. "The more you follow Christ, the more you become like him, until one day you find yourself wooden and nailed to a life you're not sure you want."

It was a stunning moment in television history. No matter what we might think of the implications of Father Ray's words, he speaks honestly about his own spiritual reality—its glory and struggle, its mingling of faith and doubt. And amid the doubt, he remains faithful. Faithful to his vows. Faithful to the God who has called him.

A lot of us harbor a deeply-rooted misconception about faithfulness. We assume that, in order to be faithful, we must rid ourselves of doubt, we must have victory over the struggle. We cite the story of Thomas, that disciple whose single claim to fame was that he doubted the resurrection. His very name is used to characterize someone who questions—a Doubting Thomas.

But Thomas wasn't the only one who doubted. He was just honest enough to verbalize his doubts. When Mary Magdalene and the other women came from the tomb on Easter morning to tell the apostles about the resurrection, the men "did not believe the woman, because their words seemed to them like nonsense" (Luke 24: 11). Even when Jesus appeared to them (Luke 24:36-37), they thought they were seeing a ghost.

Still, poor old Thomas gets the brunt of the criticism. But when he finally does see Jesus, he receives not judgement, but acceptance—and gentleness and understanding. "Put your finger here," Jesus says, "and see my hands. Reach out your hand and touch my side. Stop doubting, and believe" (John 20:27).

Stop doubting, and believe. Christ's words do not represent condemnation, but invitation. Thomas spoke his doubts openly, honestly, and Christ answered them. Jesus reached out to him and drew him in.

Faithfulness is not a matter of gritting your teeth and hanging on. It's a matter of trusting the Lord enough to be candid about your doubts. It's about having enough faith in the character of God to question.

So go ahead, ask your questions. Your faith will be stronger for it.

Friendship

*Friendship makes prosperity brilliant,
and lightens adversity by dividing it.*
— Cicero, 44 B.C.

The movie *Beaches* wasn't billed as a love story. C. C. Bloom, an outrageous child entertainer, befriends Hillary, the proper daughter of a rich business tycoon. They meet as pre-teens and see each other through three decades of turmoil. C. C. struggles to make it on Broadway, Hillary marries a man who has an affair and leaves her, pregnant and alone, to raise her daughter. Through it all, the two forge an unlikely friendship that stabilizes them and gives them hope. At the end, as Hillary is dying from cardiomyopa-thy, she is tempted to give up. She abandons care of her daughter to C. C., and then resents the close bond that forms between her child and her best friend. Finally C. C. decides to stop coddling her, and tells her, "You're not dead yet. But you might as well be, the way you're acting." Hillary rises to the challenge, rallies, and is able to spend her last days close to the two people she loves most—thanks to the honesty and faithfulness of her friend.

But *Beaches* is a love story. The kind of love that

perseveres despite terrible odds, the kind of love that speaks truth even when it hurts. In our society, we don't call it love. We call it friendship. And we sometimes assume it to be inferior to romantic love—shallower, less meaningful. Yet friendship often goes deeper than romance, for it's based not on beauty or passion or physical intimacy, but on the solid foundation of reality. A friend is one who knows the truth about you, the whole truth, and still loves you.

Jesus said that there was no greater love than the kind of friendship that would lay down its life for a friend (John 15:13). And perhaps there is no greater virtue for a woman or man to possess than the ability to be a true friend.

Friendship is an undervalued relationship in modern society. We have lots of acquaintances—people we socialize with, work with, invite to dinner, greet warmly on Sunday morning. But how many of them are true friends? How many of them can we call at four in the morning when the world caves in? How many of them know what kinds of struggles we face in the secret places of our hearts? How many know our doubts and fears? Our longings and dreams?

True friends are rare, and if we recognize their worth, we will cultivate those relationships with honesty and openness, with encouragement, affirmation, and acceptance. We will value them and give them priority in our lives. We will be there for them and allow them to be there for us as well.

Friendship mirrors the love God has for us, calling us not servants but "friends."

Generosity

Of all virtues, magnanimity is the rarest.
— William Hazlitt, 1823.

Ted Turner, the multi-billionaire who single-handedly built CNN and turned cable TV into a household necessity, has long been known for one thing: his money. But this year he made a different kind of name for himself. He pledged a billion dollars to United Nations service organizations for their charity work around the world, and he challenged other multi-millionaires to open their clenched fists and begin giving as well.

Sure, Ted Turner can afford it. After all, how much money can one man spend in a lifetime? And of course, the gesture didn't hurt his public image, either. Maybe his motives were less than pure. Maybe, as the cynics claim, he did it just to make himself look good. But one thing is certain: a lot of homeless, hungry people stand to benefit from Ted Turner's generosity.

Now, most of us don't have Ted Turner's billions. Most of us are just ordinary people juggling bills and trying to figure out a way to send the kids to college, pay the mortgage, and provide care for aging parents. But however much or little we have, if we call ourselves Christians, we have an obligation before God to be generous.

Think you have nothing to give? Think again. "You will be made rich in every way," Paul tells the church at Corinth, "so that you can be generous on every occasion, and through us your generosity will result in thanksgiving to God" (2 Cor. 9:11).

Paul doesn't say that Christians will be given great *monetary* wealth; he says that we will be "made rich in every way." Rich in love. Rich in time. Rich in creativity. Rich in compassion.

We are already a wealthy people. Maybe what we need is a redefinition of generosity.

Generosity does not depend upon the bank balance, but upon the heart. The widow at Zarephath (1 Kings 17: 7-24) who supported the prophet Elijah with her handful of flour and small cruet of oil showed great generosity. The old woman who put her two copper coins into the temple treasury (Mark 12:42-44) became Jesus' example of sacrificial giving. Jonathan demonstrated generosity when he risked his own life to save David from King Saul's anger (1 Sam. 20).

Yes, we can give money. But more importantly, we can give ourselves. We can offer our time to listen to the reminiscences of the old or kiss the scraped knees of the young. We can bind up the wounds of the broken with an hour of attention.

God has given you great wealth. Be generous with encouragement, with affirmation, with empathy, with compassion. Give freely of your time, energy, imagination, and wisdom.

You have riches to offer that can change people's lives for eternity.

Goodness

few years ago Lewis Smedes published a book entitled, *A Pretty Good Person*. I've always appreciated Smedes' work, and this title in particular intrigued me—especially the subtitle: *What it Takes to Live with Courage, Gratitude, and Integrity OR When Pretty Good Is as Good as You Can Be*. Smedes says: "The best people I know are muddling their way through a mess of moral rubbish on the steep road to character."

A lot of us Christians have a problem with the concept of "goodness." We want to be "good people," or at the very least, pretty good people. But our desire for goodness seems to butt heads with Scriptures like Romans 3:10: "There is no one righteous, not even one."

Still, we teach our children right from wrong and urge them to "be good." We describe other people, based on their behavior, as "good" or "bad." We say, of some misguided but well-meaning soul, "He has good intentions," or "She has a good heart." And we even acknowledge that goodness, at least in human terms, does not necessarily depend on faith: "She's not a Christian, but she's a good woman."

The virtue of goodness is difficult to describe. We know it when we see it, but we have a hard time defining exactly what it is that makes a person "good."

Jesus seemed to have the same problem. So he resorted to parables and images. "Every good tree bears good fruit, but a bad tree bears bad fruit" (Matt. 7:17). "The good man brings good things out of the good stored up in him, and the evil man brings evil things out of the evil stored up in him" (Matt. 12:35). Peter urged believers to "make every effort to add to your faith goodness; and to goodness, knowledge. . ." (2 Pet. 1:5), but he didn't tell us what goodness means.

Perhaps only God can evaluate the relative goodness of our hearts. Only the Lord can see, where we cannot, that the "good unbeliever" whose behavior baffles us is striving, consciously or unconsciously, toward the light of Christ. Only God can know what is in our souls, the motivation that renders our actions, in eternal terms, either "good" or "bad."

All we can see is fruit. We can see the outcome of the loving heart. We can sense the wonders of the grace-filled spirit. We can hear the good words that proceed out of a soul given to God. We can look, and listen, and touch. We can be changed. And we can draw others to the Lord by the goodness of our own lives.

Maybe the key, as Smedes implies, lies in our determination to keep "muddling through" on the "steep road to character."

And in keeping our eyes on our good, good God.

Grace

The Prodigal Son. We know the story; we've heard it preached a thousand times. How like the prodigal we are, running away from God and living in profligacy and excess. And then when we come to our senses, our loving Father is waiting on the road to welcome us home. It's a wonderful story of grace and forgiveness. It makes us feel good.

The problem is, a lot of us aren't the Prodigal at all. We are the Elder Brother, the "good kid" who stayed home and obeyed his father. And when the Prodigal returns and the fatted calf is slain, when the musicians tune their instruments and the festivities begin, we go to our rooms and pout. We grumble and complain. We say, "Hey, what about me? I've always done what you asked, and I've never been celebrated like this!"

Let's face it, it's hard sometimes to extend grace to others. It's difficult to rejoice when others receive blessing and honor, especially when we think they don't deserve it. But isn't that what grace is—a gift not based on deserving?

We struggle to reconcile the

inequities of life, when what God wants from us is surrender to the way of grace. "From the fullness of [God's] grace," John says, "we have all received one blessing after another" (John 1:16). And in response, we are called to let grace fill our hearts and overflow into our interactions with others.

Hebrews 12:15 shows us what happens when we fall prey to the Elder Brother syndrome: "See to it that no one misses the grace of God and that no bitter root grows up to cause trouble and defile many." The poor brother didn't understand that the grace and forgiveness extended to his prodigal sibling didn't deduct from his portion of his father's love. He became bitter because he couldn't comprehend the limitless supply of grace that was available.

If we want to be grace-filled people, we begin by taking a long hard look at the grace that has been extended to us. Paul called himself the "chief of sinners," the greatest example of the abounding grace of God. I have to admit, if Paul could say that about himself, what must I say about my own experience of grace? Far beyond the grace given to me in salvation, God's grace and love is poured out in my life daily. Everything is gift—the loving relationships that surround me, the call to significant work, the material provisions that meet and exceed my needs.

We have nothing to lose and everything to gain by being gracious to others who "get more than they deserve." God calls us to join the festivities, to make merry with our sisters and brothers who have, at long last, returned home.

So put on your dancing shoes. There's plenty of grace to go around.

Gratitude

The bird of paradise alights only upon the hand that does not grasp.

— John Berry, 1961

When I was little, my mother and father, like most dedicated parents of Baby Boomers, worked hard to raise me as a polite child. From the time I could speak in complete sentences, I was trained to say "Yes, sir" and "No ma'am" to my elders. And of course they drilled into me the "magic words"— *please* and *thank you.* If I wanted a cookie, I had to say "please," and when it was delivered, my mother didn't let go until the "thank you" was forthcoming.

But my parents taught me something far more important than the outward semblance of polite conversation. They also instilled in me an attitude of gratitude. And they did it by *not* giving me everything I thought I wanted, even if I said "please" and "thank you."

Gratitude—a scarce commodity in twentieth-century society—is a virtue we would do well to nurture. Life, after all, doesn't owe us happiness or contentment or personal fulfillment. These are not the *source* of gratitude, but its *results*. We become happy, spiritually prosperous people not because we receive what we want, but because we appreciate what we have.

What does it mean to cultivate a heart of gratitude? It means opening our eyes, looking around at the multitude of gifts and blessings that fill our lives. It means recognizing our family, friends, and loved ones, as aqueducts through which God's great love flows out to us. It means rejoicing in all we've been given rather than resenting what we lack.

And we are, indeed, a wealthy people. "God's divine power," Peter reminds us, "has given us everything we need for life and godliness" (2 Pet. 1:3). We have only to keep our hearts and eyes open, and we will be overwhelmed with the multitude of God's blessings.

But gratitude doesn't end with our private thanks to God. We need to show gratitude as well to those who touch our lives, who love us, minister to us, and make the world we live in a warmer, safer, kinder place.

The miracle of gratitude works both inside and out, backwards and forwards. As we express our gratefulness to the people who have given themselves to us, we minister to them and honor them for their faithfulness to God. But we also minister to ourselves. Gratitude tenderizes our hearts and makes us quicker to see and appreciate the daily gifts that come our way.

It's easy to take the gifts of life for granted, to accept them casually, as if we deserved God's generosity. But when we get a glimpse—just the tiniest glimmer—of the blessings that have been bestowed upon us, our hearts will overflow with gratitude, and our joy and contentment will spill over to those around us.

Honesty

> No legacy is so rich as honesty,
> — Shakespeare

It was a fascinating and hilarious premise for a movie: an executive for a major advertising firm, cracking under the stress of his job, has a nervous breakdown and begins to tell the truth about the products. *Volvo — it's boxy, but it runs. Diet Pepsi won't make you sexy, but it tastes pretty good.* The poor guy is institutionalized, but by mistake his ad campaigns are used and prove phenomenally successful. Such honesty in a business infamous for making false claims is refreshing — and exceptionally attractive.

Ironic, isn't it? Comedy can be based on honesty, but successful drama, to succeed, usually hinges on deception and intrigue. Maybe it's because we live in a world where honesty is such a surprise.

We know from experience, after all, that most of our politicians are accomplished liars. We watch the news and hear stories of scam artists swindling little old ladies out of their last dime. Car companies charge customers for repairs they've never made. Even doctors inflate their bills and perform unnecessary operations on patients just for the sake of the insurance payoff.

No wonder we don't trust anyone. No longer does the world run on an agreement and a handshake. Now the principle is, "Get it in writing, and get it notarized."

Honesty may seem to belong to a bygone generation, but in God's system of values it is not only the best policy, it is Christ's policy. "The Lord detests lying lips," Proverbs 12:22 says, "but he delights in [those] who are truthful."

But sometimes we get the wrong idea about truth. Sometimes we mistake truthfulness for tactless savagery, saying whatever we want to say without regard to the wounds our "truthfulness" may inflict. Telling your best friend, "Yes, that dress makes your backside look as big as a barn," is probably not quite what the Lord had in mind!

We need to understand that our commitment to honesty, first and foremost, has to do with telling *ourselves* the truth—and telling the truth *about* ourselves. If we're honest, we won't try to hide from God or from our own hearts. We won't engage in self-deception, trying to pretend we're smarter or more spiritual or more perfect than we really are. We'll allow the truth of the Holy Spirit to penetrate our souls and live in the awareness of our need for grace.

If we're honest, we won't try to put up a false front before other people. We'll speak truthfully and act with integrity. We'll honor our promises and admit our faults rather than making excuses for our behavior.

We'll trust God to handle our public image.

Hopefulness

It's been a miserable winter, at least by North Carolina standards. El Nino has brought us torrential rains, disaster-level flooding, mud slides, washed-out bridges, and one snowstorm that left 44,000 people in the country without power for days. Here in the mountains we're *ready* for spring.

And despite the waterlogged earth and the dismal gray skies, someone else is ready, too. All around the perimeter of the house, in every flower bed, the bulbs we planted last fall are pushing toward the light. Daffodil heads, still closed tight, wait for the first warmth of the sun. Iris stalks are showing. Crocuses push through the mulch.

There's hope—that poetic kind of hope that Shelley expressed so well: "O wind! If winter come, can spring be far behind?"

Well, further behind than we might like it to be. But it's coming. It always does.

"The sun will come out tomorrow," Little Orphan Annie sings in the Broadway hit. "Accen-tuate the positive," the old forties tune advises. Even Scarlett O'Hara, after losing her beloved

Tara to the Yankees, can still say, "After all, tomorrow is another day."

Hope. The promise of spring. Christians, of all people, should be people of hope. We have every reason to be optimistic, to set aside our cynicism and believe in good things to come. After all, God has promised that "hope does not disappoint us" (Rom. 5:5).

But hopefulness is by definition a future-oriented virtue. And sometimes we get so caught up in our present condition that we can't see beyond the current difficulties. The dreariness of spiritual winter has us convinced that the sun will never come out again. Our lives seem like Narnia without Aslan—"always winter but never Christmas."

If we truly desire to be hopeful people, we need to understand that faith, which is the basis for our hope, is not dependent upon

circumstances, but upon the *character* of God. When we focus on circumstances, we question the character of God. When we focus on the character of God, however, we put circumstances into their proper perspective.

God has given us the assurance that our lives—present, past, and future—are in more capable hands than our own. "'I know the plans I have for you,' declares the Lord, 'plans to prosper you and not to harm you, plans to give you hope and a future'" (Jer. 29:11).

Our parents called it optimism. Self-help groups call it positive thinking. God calls it *hope,* and tells us that when nothing else remains, this virtue, along with faith and love, will still be standing strong.

So put on your boots. Take a walk in your garden and listen to the daffodils. They whisper in the wind: Spring is coming!

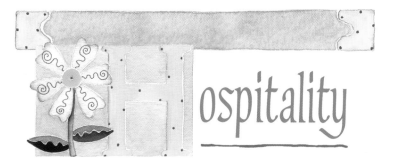

Hospitality

*A guest never forgets
the host who has treated him kindly.*
— Homer, 9th c. B.C.

I've never quite understood the Martha Stewart phenomenon. The woman is supposedly the epitome of hospitality—creative, competent, able to present a five-course dinner with a single bound. And perhaps some of her skills do foster the gift of hospitality. But some of the things she does simply baffle me.

Ornamental angels made from pine cones? Homemade marshmallows? I'll admit I've never had the pleasure of tasting a homemade marshmallow, but why would anyone spend half a day in the kitchen making something you can buy in a bag for eighty-five cents?

I'm willing to admit that hospitality is a virtue. But from the Martha Stewart perspective, it's just not one I happen to possess.

But maybe I'm being a little too narrow with my definition of hospitality. In biblical times, hospitality was a matter of life and death. God's people were commanded to be hospitable to strangers—to provide food and water and shelter to them, lest they die in the hostile desert climate.

In Deuteronomy 23:3-4, God instructed that the Moabites be excluded from the assembly of believers because they did not bring food and water to the Israelites when they came out of captivity in Egypt. But later a Moabite woman named Ruth redeemed her people's reputation by her obedience to God and her loyal service to her mother-in-law, Naomi.

I'd like to think that God's definition of hospitality—rather than being limited to gourmet dinner parties—extends to the care and nurture of souls. To those times when we set aside our own agenda to put on a pot of coffee and listen to the struggles of a sister or brother who's going through a hard time. To the hours we spend on the phone comforting a grieving friend.

These are the life-and-death matters of modern society. For the most part, the people who travel through our daily lives aren't in danger of dying from exposure or malnutrition or dehydration. But they do need spiritual sustenance—the bread of truth, the water of grace, the encompassing shelter of God's love.

"Do not forget to entertain strangers," Hebrews 13:2 reminds us, "for by so doing some people have entertained angels without knowing it."

No, Martha Stewart I am not. I can barely cook, and I'm not very adept at entertaining large groups of people. But I like to believe that somewhere along the way I've given comfort to an angel or two—or at least weary souls who needed a safe place to rest on their journey through the wilderness.

Joyfulness

True joy is the earnest which we have of heaven,
it is the treasure of the soul,
and therefore should be laid in a safe place,
and nothing in this world is safe to place it in.

— John Donne, 1625

Yesterday was Ash Wednesday. A small group of us gathered in the sanctuary as darkness fell outside, preparing to receive the traditional imposition of ashes and celebrate communion together.

The forty days of Lent is often perceived as a dark time in the church year. A time to reflect upon the suffering of Christ, to make a symbolic sacrifice as a reminder of the Lord's ultimate sacrifice for us. A time to think about sin.

But as I stood and walked down the aisle to receive the ashen sign of the cross upon my forehead—ashes created from the burning of palms from the last Easter season—my mind was not on sin or suffering or darkness. I was focused only on the words of the pastor as he dipped his finger in the ash. He called each person by name and said, "The old has passed away, and all things have become new."

What a powerful testimony of joy! Yes, life is difficult. Yes, we struggle with sin and self-denial. But no matter what trials assail us, no matter what sorrow of the soul comes upon us, we have this assurance: In Christ, the old has passed away, and all things have become new.

True joy, the kind of joy that endures despite all odds, is not founded on circumstance, but on the faithfulness of God. Happiness, that elusive state of feeling good about ourselves, comes and goes. When relationships are healthy, when love abounds, when the checking account is solvent, when we like our jobs and find peace at home, it's easy enough to be happy. But when the mortgage is due and there's no money in the bank, when our kids rebel and our spouses withdraw, when home is a place of chaos rather than harmony, happiness dissolves like an ice cube on a hot griddle.

Godly joy however, is not so ephemeral. "Though the fig tree does not bud and there are no grapes on the vine, though the olive crop fails and the fields produce no food, though there are no sheep in the pen and no cattle in the stalls, yet I will rejoice in the Lord, I will be joyful in God my Savior" (Hab. 3:17-18).

We are called to be joyful people. "Be joyful always," Paul instructs us, "for this is God's will for you in Christ Jesus" (1 Thess. 5:16-18).

How can we be "joyful always"? By keeping our eyes focused on God, who is the source of our faith. By trusting the Lord's love and grace and goodness when the fig tree does not blossom and the cattle pens are empty. By looking beyond our circumstances to the faithfulness of the One who called us—to rejoice.

Kindness

That best portion of a good man's life,
His little, nameless, unremembered acts
Of kindness and of love,

~ William Wordsworth, 1798

Ronny was running the race of his life, The Special Olympics, with his mom and dad and hundreds—maybe thousands—of people watching from the stands. He could see the finish line, and no one was ahead of him. His friend Joey stood at the line, clapping and yelling, urging him on.

Then Ronny turned and looked over his shoulder. A boy named Curtis, the new friend Ronny had met just that morning, was right behind him and gaining ground. At that moment, to Ronny's horror, Curtis stumbled and went down.

Ronny stopped in his tracks. He looked at the finish line, then back at Curtis. And without a second thought he turned back, helped Curtis to his feet, and together, with their arms around

each other's shoulders, they crossed the finish well back in the pack.

"Why did you stop?" someone asked. "You could have finished first and won the race."

But Ronny didn't care. He grinned and gave Curtis a big hug. "We won," he said. "We both won."

Whatever his limitations, Ronny comprehended something essential about life. He understood that winning isn't the most significant thing in the world. That being kind is important, even if you lose the race.

Remember the Good Samaritan? He had nothing to gain and everything to lose when he stopped to help that mugging victim. He was a hated Samaritan, an outcast. The religious people had all passed by. Still, he showed kindness. He went out of his way, spent his own money, rearranged his busy schedule, to help a man he had never met. And Jesus used him, not the religious leaders, as the example of neighborly kindness and compassion (Luke 10:29-37).

A few years ago a bumper sticker appeared, generated by the popularity of a new book. *Practice Random Acts of Kindness*, it said. And I suppose a random act of kindness is better than none at all. But God calls us to more than random kindness. God calls us to *clothe* ourselves with it, to wrap it around us so that kindness is the first thing people touch when they reach in our direction.

Love

Love is a great thing, a great good in every wise.
—Thomas a' Kempis, 1426

Valentine's Day has come and gone. My friend the florist worked forty-five hours in three days, trying in vain to fill all the last-minute orders for sweetheart roses. The card shops and candy counters look as if Moses' plague of locusts had come through. For one more year, we have celebrated love.

But although St. Valentine has been adopted as the patron saint of lovers, the Feast of St. Valentine has nothing to do with candy hearts or roses or romantic dinners. Valentine, a third-century martyr, was beheaded for his faith on February 14, 269 A.D. History records little about him except that he was both a priest and a physician—and thus probably merited his canonization through a life of good works. He died for love, but not the kind of love we celebrate.

He died because he loved God more than life.

The society in which we live is obsessed with romance—or, more specifically, with sex. We are bombarded on all sides with romantic imagery—some positive, some negative, but all centering on only one kind of love. Eros. Physical love. Sensuality. Anyone looking on would think, literally, that "love makes the world go 'round."

Well, *love* does make the world go 'round. But not that kind of love. *Agape* love, God's selfless love, set the world in motion and keeps the stars in place. Christ, the Creator's Love incarnate, is the source and center of the universe—in Christ "all things hold together" (Col. 1:15-17).

No matter what the world may try to tell us, God's love is the foundation for all other loves. We as Christians are called to "love as the Lord loved us,"—that is, selflessly, sacrificially. To offer ourselves to others as God offered Christ to us.

True love, the God-like kind of love, does not bargain or manipulate or seek to control. It gives itself freely as a gift, not as a bribe for something in return. Real love has its beginning and its consummation in the Divine.

Two hundred years after the resurrection, a man named Valentine bared his neck on the chopping block for love. Not the love of a woman, or the love of an idea, or the love of a philosophy—but for the love of Christ, who had already sacrificed life for love.

Perhaps it's time for us as Christians to reclaim love and bring it back where it belongs—to wrestle it away from the songwriters and the movie producers and the greeting card vendors and return it, worn and battered as it might be, to the lap of God. Perhaps it is time for us to do a little re-evaluation of our own loves, and bring them, too, under the canopy of God's grace.

Meekness

*If thou have any good things,
believe better things of others,
that thou may keep thy meekness.*
— Thomas à Kempis, 1426

I grew up in church and Sunday School. I heard lessons on the Beatitudes, even memorized them. "Blessed are the meek," Jesus said, "for they shall inherit the earth." But in the real world, meekness did not seem to be a virtue. Nobody got anything without staking a claim to it. The meek were weak, spineless, doormats who let other people walk all over them.

Then, midway into my twenties, I read Numbers 12:3: "Now the man Moses was very meek, above all the men which were upon the face of the earth" (KJV).

Moses? Meek? It must be a typographical error. Surely not Moses, the great Deliverer of Israel, who called down fiery hail and plagues of frogs to liberate God's people from Egyptian rule? Surely not Moses, who lifted his rod and parted the sea, delivered water from the rock, stood before God and brought the Commandments down from

Mount Sinai? If Moses was the meekest person who ever lived, I had to do some serious redefining of my concept of meekness.

Then I took another look at Moses—specifically that fascinating scene at the Burning Bush. Chosen to bear the news of liberation to God's people, Moses asked the Lord to choose someone else—not because he was a weakling or a coward, but because he knew his own limitations. He was no good at public speaking, he protested. How could he stand before Pharaoh and demand that he let God's people go? How could he, for that matter, even convince his own people that God had sent him?

Moses knew himself. He was aware of his strengths and weaknesses. And yet, when God called him, he removed his shoes and bowed down in obedience.

Meekness is the outward manifestation of humility, the active response of a soul committed to God's purposes. The heart that knows its dependence upon God can strike bravely into the unknown, counting always on his faithfulness to provide whatever is needed.

We don't have to be afraid of our shortcomings. They are as much a part of God's plan as our strengths and gifts. If we held within ourselves all that was necessary to fulfill his purpose, we wouldn't need the miracle of God's presence.

The place where you stand—wherever the Lord has put you—is holy ground.

Take off your shoes. Bow down.

Acknowledge your limitations, and trust God to be God.

Mercy

It happened in the sixties, but I remember it as if it were yesterday—the horrifying picture on the nightly news of a Buddhist priest striking a match and setting himself on fire in the market square. It was an act of self-sacrifice, an offering of the body for the salvation of the soul.

We as Christians shrink from such images, yet, in spiritual terms, we do the same thing all the time. We sacrifice ourselves on the altar of Christian duty. We pour ourselves out, heart, mind, and soul, as if our eternal destiny depended upon the depth of our exhaustion.

God, however, is more merciful than we are. "I desire mercy, not sacrifice, and acknowledgment of God rather than burnt offerings" (Hosea 6:6).

Certainly, our invitation to follow Christ includes a call to action. We are instructed to feed the hungry, clothe the naked, give shelter to the homeless, defend widows and orphans, minister to the imprisoned. We are challenged to live the truth even as we preach it. But we are not called to sacrifice ourselves upon the altar, or to demand such sacrifice from others.

What does the Lord require of us? "To act justly and to love mercy and to walk humbly with your God" (Mic. 6:8).

We live in a merciless world— a society of ever-increasing expectation. We're pushed to do more, to produce more, to make more money, to meet higher goals. And we transfer those expectations to our Christian lives. We say yes to everything. We demand that our pastors be superhuman, our youth leaders miracle-workers. We drive them, and ourselves, into therapy or collapse or rage.

We need a little mercy. We need to concede our own human-ness and that of our sisters and brothers. Once and for all, we need to realize that God does not want our sacrifices and our burnt-out offerings. The sacrifice of Christ was sufficient.

In modern terms, mercy means cutting ourselves and others a little slack. Admitting our human limitations. Taking a little time off. Giving ourselves and those around us the opportunity to refresh and regroup, to draw on the healing, restorative power offered to us in Jesus Christ. We are weary people, in need of God's rest. And the Lord has provided it for us if we'll only get down off the altar for a minute.

God calls it Sabbath. Mercy, not sacrifice. Awareness of God rather than burnt offerings.

God is Lord of the resting time.

Patience

Patience is a bitter plant but it has a sweet fruit.
— German Proverb

The old professor sat in his office, surrounded by papers that needed grading and piles of mid-term exams. He had been trying for weeks to finish an article for a scholarly journal, and the outline still sat next to his typewriter, untouched.

A knock sounded on the door, and he shook his head impatiently. Why couldn't he get a few moments of peace? Just a little time to finish that article and catch up on his paperwork . . .

He sighed and said, "Come in."

The door opened to reveal a young woman—a student in one of his classes. She was a bright girl, with a promising future, but she needed some direction. "Am I interrupting your work?" she asked timidly, staring around at the mass of unfinished work that cluttered the office. "I could come back some other time."

The professor looked into her face and saw that familiar expression of hope and anticipation. And suddenly he remembered why he had gone into teaching in the first place. "Yes, you're interrupting," he said. "But come in. Interruptions *are* my work."

We are an impatient people, even those of us who claim the name of Christ. We have a hard time seeing beyond our schedules, our responsibilities, our well-ordered plans and goals.

Patience is the kind of character trait that everyone wants to possess but no one wants to develop. And it's no wonder. The Bible tells us that suffering brings patience, (Rom. 5:3) so we don't dare pray for patience lest suffering come. The truth is, we want what we want when we want it. We don't like sitting in traffic. We're frustrated and demoralized by delayed gratification and unanswered prayer. We want patience, but we want it *right now*.

But patience is, by its very nature, a future-oriented virtue.

"If we hope for what we do not yet have," Romans 8:25 tells us, "we wait for it patiently." Hebrews encourages us to "imitate those who through faith and patience inherit what has been promised" (Heb. 6:12).

Patience, it seems, is developed in the Christian life through two processes—*delay* and *interruption*. Neither is very attractive to goal-driven, product-oriented twentieth century people like us. But our responses to both are based on faith. Faith in God's timing, and faith in God's priority system.

If we want to be people of patience, we need to trust that God is in control of the outcome. What we call a detour may be the Lord's scenic turnpike. When our plans are delayed by gridlock or interrupted by unanticipated re-routing, God knows the best way home.

Penitence

God offers to every mind its choice
between truth and repose.

—Emerson, 1841

Remember the movie *Love Story*—that tear-jerking tale of young love that overcomes all odds and then ends in a noble, heart-wrenching death? You may not recall the details, but you're sure to remember the one line from the movie that makes most people laugh. The boy has done something stupid—I forget what—and hurt the girl he supposedly loves. So he comes to her and says, "I'm sorry." But before he can even get the apology out, she stops him.

"Don't," she says. "Don't say it. Love means never having to say you're sorry."

And just what kind of love would that be?

It's a sweet, sappy sentiment, to be sure, but it's utter nonsense. Love—whether it's with your spouse, your kids, your parents, your best friend, or your God—means you'd better learn to say "I'm sorry." And fast. Penitence is the cornerstone of real relationship.

Take David, for example. The King of all Israel. A person of power, wealth, and influence. A fellow the Bible calls "a man after God's own heart" (Acts 13:22). But David was far from sinless. In 2 Samuel 11, David lusts after Bathsheba, has her husband Uriah killed off in battle, and then takes her for his own. In the very next chapter, the prophet Nathan confronts the king with his sin.

Well, David loved God, but he evidently didn't subscribe to the "love means never having to say you're sorry" school of theology. When Nathan reveals his sin, David doesn't try to squirm out of it, make excuses, or offer rationalizations. He says, simply and directly, "I have sinned against the Lord" (2 Sam. 12:13). David's sin is forgiven, even though he has to live with the consequences he has brought upon himself.

The virtue of penitence doesn't mean that we grovel in despair and make sin our primary focus in life. But it does mean that we stand ready and willing to own up to our sin, whether we have violated our relationship with God or offended someone else.

We don't need to confess for God's sake, of course. The Lord already knows far more than we do about what's in our hearts, and the sacrifice of Christ has already paid the penalty. But for our own sakes—and for the sake of others we may have hurt or betrayed—we need to come clean about it. Rationalization doesn't cleanse the soul; excuses do not mend the heart. What we hide festers and contaminates us. What we reveal purifies and heals.

Love means never having to say you're sorry? I don't think so.

Real love means being willing to say it whenever necessary, as often as necessary. Those three little words—*I love you*—are rendered even more powerful by three more: *I was wrong.*

Respect

*If you have respect for people as they are,
you can be more effective in helping them
to become better than they are.*
— John W. Gardner, 1968

A few years ago, I went car shopping. I had a model all picked out, and I had enough money in my checking account to pay cash on the spot.

But the salesman shot himself in the foot. He made a point of showing me the lighted vanity mirror and the cup holders, then turned condescending when I raised questions about engine size and power and fuel economy. As if I wouldn't know the difference, he quoted me a trade value less than half what my old car was really worth. And then he sealed his fate. He said, "Well, honey, bring your husband back to approve it and we'll talk about a deal."

Aretha Franklin made a fortune out of a single word: "R-E-S-P-E-C-T," she sang. "Find out what it means to me. All I ask from you is just a little respect...."

Why, other than Aretha's obvious talent, was the song "Respect" such an enormous hit? I think it was because she touched a nerve in many women—the desire to be respected rather than just wanted. That was the quality the doomed car salesman lacked. And, if truth be told, the virtue that many of us as Christians neglect when we seek to minister to those around us.

God has called us to reach out to others, to be agents of reconciliation to a troubled, dying world. The problem is, we sometimes approach the troubled and dying as if we have all the answers, and they've never even considered the right questions.

That's not the way God intends for us to reach out. First Peter 3:15 admonishes us. "Always be prepared to give an answer to everyone who asks you to give the reason for the hope that you have. But do this with gentleness and respect."

We show disrespect to others when we insult them by our know-it-all, holier-than-thou attitudes. We disrespect them when we belittle their faith, or lack of it. We disrespect them when we demean their suffering, ignore their honest questions, tell them just to believe and stop doubting.

Now, we don't do it deliberately; we're not always conscious of being disrespectful. But if we want to meet people where they are and help them to find direction and guidance, we need to be conscious. Conscious of the way Christ dealt with others, of his tenderness and acceptance. Conscious that he, who knew much more than we do about the human heart, allowed people to find their own way to faith.

Respect draws people to the truth. When we respect them, amid all their doubts and struggles, we give them the liberty to make their own decisions in their own time. When we honor their search, we honor the image of Christ within them. And we demonstrate our own trust in God, who is capable of leading people where they need to go.

Righteousness

*What is the freedom of the most free?
To do what is right!*

— Goethe, 1788

In a shocking, thought-provoking episode of the legal drama, *The Practice*, a neighborhood association brings a lawsuit against the government. The high-power lines that run through their neighborhood have resulted in a cancer cluster. Leukemia, lung cancer, breast cancer, brain tumors — nearly every house on the block has at last one family member who has been diagnosed.

Everyone, even the lawyers for the plaintiffs, realize there is no case. They cannot *prove* that the power lines caused the cancer. But for the individuals involved, it's a matter of principle — to make the government face the results of its negligence. They're bound to lose, but even so, the public will be made aware of the dangers.

Then the verdict comes in: a staggering and unexpected judgment for the plaintiffs, a victory to the tune of forty million dollars. The little guy has finally won.

But the judge, exercising his judicial privilege, overturns the verdict and finds in favor of the defendants. The plaintiffs, despite their emotional appeal, have not proved their case. The government doesn't have to pay a dime.

It's the *right* verdict, according to the law. But not the *righteous* one.

Being right isn't the same thing as being righteous. The Pharisees found that out the hard way when they tried to justify themselves as keepers of the law. "The truth will set you free," Jesus told them (John 8: 31). But they couldn't get their minds around the concept. They were children of Abraham; they didn't need to be set free.

The local rumor mill, clearly, had done its work. Wasn't this Jesus the one born out of wedlock? Who was he to be telling them that they needed to be set free? Who was the righteous one here? "Abraham is *our* father," they sneered. "*We* are not illegitimate children."

And the Pharisees were right—at least technically. They were, indeed, descendants of the patriarchs; they kept the law; they could claim Abraham as their father. But Jesus was talking about a different kind of parentage—the legacy of the soul, the inheritance that comes through faith.

The Pharisees kept the Jewish commandments religiously, every jot and tittle. But they were not righteous in God's sight. Righteousness is a matter of the heart, not the mind. It is based on faith, on surrender to the truth, not on keeping the law.

The virtue of righteousness is the state of being in right relationship, vertically with God and then horizontally with those around us. If we're righteous, we are liberated by the truth rather than being constrained by legalism. And yes, we "do right," but as an outgrowth of our relationships with God and others, not as proof of our adherence to the law.

Servanthood

The noblest service comes from nameless hands, and the best servant does his work unseen.
— Oliver Wendell Holmes, Sr., 1872

The world is full of invisible people.

All those workers behind the scenes who make things run. The secretary who does the work of a dozen executives and makes her boss look like a genius. The teenager who mows the church lawn, shovels snow, and helps in the nursery on Sunday morning. The little old lady, nearly eighty years old, who runs a soup kitchen for the homeless. The nameless servant who makes coffee for every fellowship hour.

Modern society values fame. Adulation comes to those who live in the spotlight—movie stars and rock musicians and football heroes. These are the "important people," the ones we look up to and emulate. But God has a different value system. God's applause is reserved for the invisible ones.

Jesus showed us the way. On the night before he was betrayed, he met with his disciples to celebrate the Passover. But before the feast began, he took water and a towel, knelt at every place at the table, and washed his followers' dirty feet. "I have set you an example," Jesus said, "that you should do as I have done for you. I tell you the truth, no servant is greater than his master" (John 13:15-16).

Christ calls us to servant-hood. To wash feet, to get dirt under our fingernails, to take up the mundane, thankless tasks that no one else wants to do. But it's hard to be a servant in a world that values celebrity. It's hard to give ourselves to invisi-bility when we'd love to see our name in lights.

Paul tells us that Christ, "being in very nature God, did not consider equality with God something to be grasped, but made himself nothing, taking the very nature of a servant.... He humbled himself and became obedient to death, even death on a cross" (Phil. 2:6-8). Make no mistake—Christ, too, was tempt-ed by the seduction of stardom. The devil offered him fame and fortune, all the kingdoms of the world, even a way out of the suffering that was to come (Luke

4:1-13). And Jesus turned him down.

How did Jesus do it? John gives us a tiny clue hidden in this passage: "Jesus knew that the Father had put all things under his power, and that he had come from God and was returning to God" (John 13: 3).

Christ understood who he was, where he had come from, and where he was going.

These are the keys to ser-vanthood. If we're confident of our place in God's family, we don't have to make a name for ourselves. If we're assured that we come from God and are called by God, we can be content to be invisible. If we are certain that our future lies with God, we don't have to exalt ourselves, for our ultimate exal-tation is already accomplished in Jesus Christ.

Trust

Strong Son of God, immortal Love ...
We that have not seen thy face, By faith, and faith
alone embrace, Believing where we cannot prove.

Alfred, Lord Tennyson, 1849

In the action-packed movie *Indiana Jones and the Last Crusade*, Indiana's quest is to find the Holy Grail, the original chalice used by Christ at the Last Supper. But in order to prove himself pure in heart, Indy must face life-threatening challenges that test his humility, his obedience, and his trust.

In the final challenge, Indy finds himself teetering on the brink of a deep, vast chasm. The way across, according to the legends, lies right before him. But he cannot see it. He must step out in faith, with no tangible assurance of support. He must trust what his eyes cannot see.

Fearful but determined, Indy steps out ... and discovers himself standing on a bridge of rock, solid and firm beneath his feet but invisible to the eye.

Seeing is believing, the world tries to tell us. But not to God. From a faith perspective, believing is seeing.

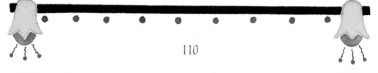

The Bible is full of exhortations to trust. "Command those who are rich in this present world not to be arrogant nor to put their hope in wealth, which is so uncertain, but to put their hope in God," Paul tells Timothy (1 Tim. 6:17). And for the church in Rome, Paul prays: "May the God of hope fill you with all joy and peace as you trust in him, so that you may overflow with hope by the power of the Holy Spirit" (Rom. 15:13).

The power of trust lies in the ability to turn over control of our lives and our destiny to One who knows far more about the future than we do. It's not weakness to trust, but strength of spirit. It is not naivete, but the utmost wisdom. For God is trustworthy. Even if we are faithless, 1 Timothy 2:13 says, God remains faithful, for the Lord cannot act contrary to the Divine Nature.

Trust in God sets us free to live authentically, to act courageously, to forgive readily. It gives us the power we need to persevere, to repent, to obey, to show compassion, to treat those around us with tolerance and respect. Trust infuses hope and joy into our daily interactions, honesty into our dealings, patience into our waiting. Trust gives us power to commit our way to One who sees the path around the bend.

If you trust, you won't be sorry.

Step out onto the invisible bridge.

God is waiting on the other side with wonders your heart cannot begin to imagine.

Love Virtue, she alone is free

She can teach ye how to climb

Higher than the sphery chime;

Or, if Virtue feeble were,

Heav'n itself would stoop to her.

———————

–John Milton, 1634

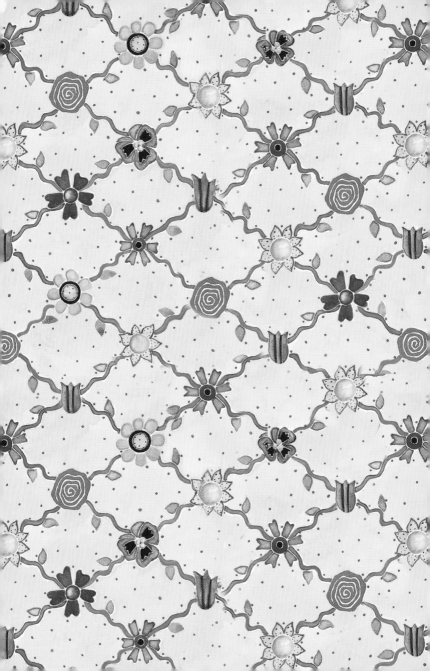

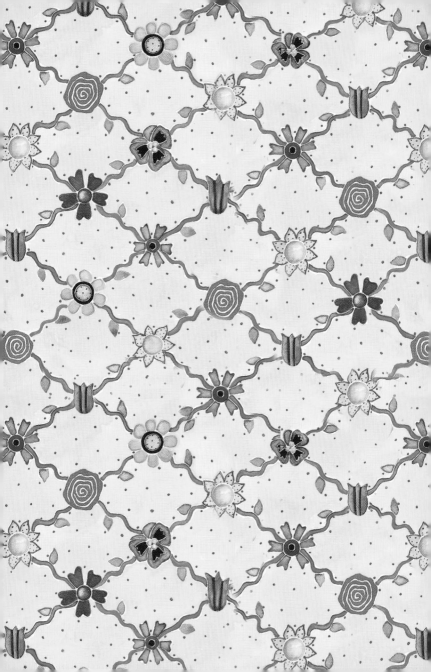